Slip of the Tongue

Slip of the Tongue
Talking about Language

Katie Haegele

First printing, September 1, 2014
All text is © Katie Haegele, 2014
This edition is © by Microcosm Publishing, 2014

Microcosm Publishing
2752 N Williams Ave
Portland, OR 97227

In the Real World series

For a catalog, write or visit
MicrocosmPublishing.com

ISBN 9781621060116
This is Microcosm #133

Edited by Erik Spellmeyer and Lauren Hage
Designed by Joe Biel
Cover by Meggyn Pommerleau

Distributed in the United States and Canada by Independent Publishers
Group and in Europe by Turnaround.

This book was printed on post-consumer paper by union workers in the
United States.

Some of these pieces originally appeared in *Bitch* magazine, the *Minneapolis
Star-Tribune*, the *Pennsylvania Gazette*, *The Philadelphia Independent*, the
Philadelphia Inquirer, *Philadelphia Weekly*, Powells.com and the *Utne Reader*.
See? No Oxford Comma needed.

Slip of the Tongue

Talking About Language

Katie Haegele

Introduction

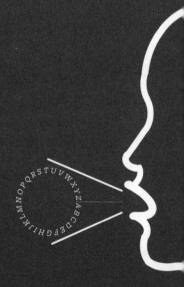

I am a little bit obsessed with Helen Keller, and I have been for a long time. I don't remember how old I was when I first read or heard her story, only that it was either in school or in the theater, when my parents took us to see *The Miracle Worker*, the stage play based on Keller's autobiography. Her story has been retold in various ways many times, to the point that it feels, to me, like Greek mythology or something biblical, like it's always been there, a book of lessons for us to learn from. One of these lessons is surely about the unruliness of the human spirit, the strength of the will to survive and thrive. But to me the important lesson—intricately bound up with that drive to live—has always been about the power of the word.

The Miracle Worker focuses on the early part of Keller's life, starting with her unusually difficult babyhood. As an infant she got seriously ill with what was probably scarlet fever or meningitis and, as everyone who has ever heard of her knows, it left her deaf and blind. Her parents didn't know that she couldn't see or hear at first because she was too little to have learned to speak, and she cried like any other baby. I remember finding that scary, the idea that you could be trapped in darkness and silence and be all the more alone because no one even knew you were stuck there. You wouldn't even know yourself, not really.

But still, she had to learn to negotiate the world of the seeing and hearing. When Helen was ten years old, her teacher Anne Sullivan came to live with the family. The young woman was mostly blind herself and had learned sign language from a classmate at the Perkins School for the Blind who also had deafness. She used signing with Helen by spelling out the signs on the palm of Helen's hand, because of course, she couldn't see them. Now here is the important part of the story: Helen didn't know what Miss Sullivan was doing. How could she? She'd never spoken with anyone, never witnessed language being used. (She had made up a kind of signing that she used to communicate with the daughter of the family cook, a girl close to her own age, but they weren't signs that corresponded to individual things and ideas. They were more like gestures, in the way that you can manage to make yourself understood by someone whose language you don't speak and who doesn't speak yours.)

The salient part of this unusual language acquisition story is that Helen didn't know that everything in the world had a name. Miss Sullivan needed to make her understand this before she could teach her anything else, so she put a doll in Helen's arms and, using the American manual alphabet, spelled out the word for doll. She did the same with a drinking cup and the table it sat on, and on herself ("Annie," "teacher"), and all that happened was that Helen got frustrated and annoyed. I remember in the play, her hair was all long and tangled and it hung in front of her face; she grunted too. She was like a wild child, locked away from human society because she couldn't communicate. It took months of persistent teaching for any understanding to break through. At the water pump, as the cold shining stream surged over her hands, Helen at once understood that the thing being signed to her was the word for water, and the reason it was different from all the other movements the woman had made with her hands was that everything has its own word. Everything has a name. There is a way to match up our lived experience with our desire—our need—to share it with each other, and that way is words.

It would be hard to exaggerate how excited I was to watch Helen understand this for the first time, and the fact that her first word was water only seemed to highlight how elemental her discovery was. The thing is, it was the first time I understood it, too. All words are signs. They're arbitrary. The word for water could sound any number of different ways (and does, in languages all over the world). But most of us learn language when we're so little that we don't remember learning it, which means we never have to think about the fact that, at one time, someone just made those words up. It's in our nature to talk about the world around us, whether we see things with our eyesight or by touch or in some other way, so we absorb language without even trying. And in all this time, the fact of that—that effortlessness—has not stopped seeming beautiful and miraculous to me. I imagine I'd feel the same way about the other functions of our bodies, if I understood them better: the elegant mechanism of an elbow swiveling in its hinge, or the tunnels and tubes that allow us to breathe and cry and, yes, to speak. If using language is a way for us humans to make sense of our world then thinking about language is the way I make sense of my humanity. There are other doors that open onto that same room: sexuality, art, religion, food. But language is the part of our lives that's always mattered to me the most, and I've written about it a lot over the years, in one way or another.

For these reasons, it's weird for me to report that I don't find writing easy to do, not even a little. I don't even really enjoy doing it most of the time. I can't think of many things that satisfy me as completely as expressing precisely what I want to say, but getting there is hard. For brief moments I'm able to capture the wonder and pain of my puny experience, using only words—the same words I use to scold my cat or tell my sister what time the movie starts—and then, just as quickly, it gets away from me again.

Contents

Section
One

Essays

1.

Either You Have It Or You Don't

After my father died, I moved back home with my mother, and during the five years that I stayed there, our little family slowly shifted around his not being there anymore, like grass growing in on an empty lot where a house used to be. Even the physical space around us altered, bit by bit, to reflect my mother's taste and not his. Outside of the fantastic pumpkin color on the dining room walls that only he knew would turn out right, there wasn't a whole lot of evidence that he had ever existed.

But I still remember this one thing that hung around for a while, and kept popping up to surprise me. When my sister was in high school she went to Disneyland with her friends, and she brought back the same gift for each of us: big coffee mugs with Disney characters on them, each personifying a different word, which was scribbled loudly all over it in different crazy fonts. My mom's word was lovely, mine was vivacious, and my dad's was pizzazz. I remember being struck at the time by the dual unlikelinesses of both stupid Disney and my very quiet sister— who is so nonverbal that she didn't even really start talking until she was 5—having come up with such a perfect word to describe him. My dad, who kept his father's fedora in his office because he knew it was cool, even if no one else did. Who stood in the laundry room, his sweaty clothes stained with green grass juice after every maniacal "aerobic gardening" session, and pulled off layer after layer of them while my mom bitched at him to get upstairs if he was gonna get undressed. Who explained to me one day when I was around nine why Buster Keaton was both funnier and sadder than Charlie Chaplin—"but maybe it's toss-up," he concluded by the end. Who let me shine up his giant hard black work shoes with this special shoe polishing kit every morning before work, even though he usually didn't have time and leather shoes, as I now know, do not need to be covered in fresh shoeblack every day to stay looking nice. The kit was a wooden box with a foot-shaped foot rest nailed to the top at an angle. Inside the box, which opened on a hinge and fastened shut with a latch, was a rag, a brush with black bristles and a couple of round tins of polish. When you opened the box it smelled tangy and toxic—I can almost taste it, remembering it now—and no one else's dad had one just like it.

As I say, after he died my mom gave away, threw away, or packed away almost all of his things. But for some reason that fucking mug stayed in the kitchen, right in the cabinet we used the most. No one could use it; no one could even touch it. But every so often in the post-dishwasher shuffle it got pushed to the front and when I'd come down in the morning and open up the cabinet while I was still groggy and in need of coffee, I'd accidentally grab it and get this quick, deep pang of yearning in my middle, the kind you get when you're stopped in your tracks at the sound of your ex's voice coming out of the answering machine.

It's that word. It's just so perfect. That's why it killed me, every single time.

Its first appearance during the glamorous 1930s. Its origin unknown. Its made-up sound, like it could be the name of a spice—an unusual one that you couldn't spell with confidence, not one you'd keep on hand but would have to go out and get special because the recipe called for it.

Those two sets of z's. What kind of word is so sure of itself that it expects you to spell it with four z's? One with pizzazz, that's for sure.

But it's a difficult word in this day and age. You can't use it very often; it's too flamboyant, too old-fashioned, too absurd. You choose it with care and use it only because it's just the right word for what you want to say. There are other words like that, of course, but none of them leap to mind.

But they wouldn't, would they?

2.

It's All A Diary

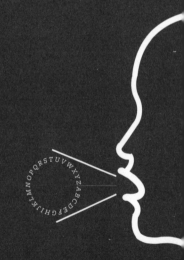

You're probably embarrassed by it, but I love your handwriting. It's a part of your body, your self, and even if I'd never met you I could get a good feeling for your physical presence by reading the words you wrote in your own hand, rather than with a machine.

You know Lynda Barry, right? The comics artist? She's put out a few unusual books in the last few years, these large not-really-comics books called *Picture This, What It Is*, and *Blabber Blabber Blabber*. In them, she talks about her relationship to art and the imagination. Rather than panels of comic strips, each page is a large painting or collage, and many of the pages stand alone as beautiful, strange paintings. Read the books as a whole, though, and you'll see a narrative take shape. This is Barry's story of how she became an artist. She talks about how her imagination works best, what she does when she's in a bad place with her work, things like that. And at one point in *Picture This* she writes that although she'd often used brushes to paint, she had never tried using them to write words. She was writing a novel on her computer, typing and deleting things over and over until she felt hopelessly stuck, and it occurred to her to try writing the book with a paintbrush, one word at a time. This she found meditative and effective, and the words began to come more easily. She says: "It took a long time to realize that I didn't need to be in the mood to move my brush before I picked it up. All I needed to do was move the brush and my mood would follow the trail."

This felt true and important to me when I read it, because I have experienced something similar, and similarly exciting, myself. I have composed articles, essays, and poems in different ways: by hand in notebooks, on typewriters, and on a computer keyboard. When I've written things by hand or on the computer it's usually out of convenience or necessity. I find it easier to jot down ideas in a small notebook that I can carry in my bag than to lug around my laptop everywhere I go, but I find it easier to compose longer pieces at my computer because it's faster and I've become accustomed to doing it this way over the years. The typewriter I've used as an experiment or for the aesthetic, because I like the jangly, messier way it can look better than the polished sameness of all computer print-outs everywhere. But what's been interesting to me is the way the words come to me differently when I use these different tools. It takes me longer to write by hand, which seems to coax forth different words altogether, and the sentences form in a different way than they would if I were using a keyboard, which allows my hands to nearly keep up with my brain. I end up saying something different when I write in different ways.

My interest in handwriting predates this discovery, and it has more to do with other people than with myself. I have saved almost every note and letter that's ever been sent to me. They fill and overflow several cardboard boxes in my hall closet, and it is because they were written or signed by people who care about me that they are worth so much to me. I even have a plastic pencil case from the seventh or eighth grade that is stuffed with little notes that were passed to me in class, all of them decorated with different colored highlighters and folded into tight thick triangles. Some of those notes are more than 20 years old, and I don't plan on getting rid of them anytime soon. When I take them out of their case and unfold and reread them, it's like I'm there again: The kids' handwriting is personal and quirky, immediate and visceral, and it paves a way into memories that still live in my mind but that I don't always have access to. Looking at her bubbly, round writing in pink and purple pen brings me Mandy, in all her fanciful loneliness, her brushed-smooth but still-lank long brown hair. I can see her. When I look at the notes from Jane, which she wrote in her grown-up, attractive, skritchy, old-fashioned cursive, I can see her in the schoolyard, talking to me quietly and seriously as we sit against the brick wall of the firehouse next door, our legs stretched out in front of us. Green-plaid skirts and navy blue knee socks, not pulled up to our knees but scrunched down around our ankles, the "cool" way. I can see the boys getting red in the face as they play kickball and box-ball and eventually roof one of the balls so they have to ask the skinny custodian, Jim Rooney, to go up on the ladder and retrieve it. I can feel myself, sitting on a hard wooden chair in a stuffy room staring at the blackboard for what seemed like forever, forever ago.

Yes, it's possible I've romanticized all this a little. Old classroom things, artifacts from my own childhood, they are fetish objects to me, it's true. But that doesn't mean they don't also have real value.

Not long ago a young curator asked me to participate in a group art show she was putting on in Philadelphia, and I decided I wanted to make something that related to handwriting. I ended up making an interactive exhibit that encouraged people to sit down and write something, anything. I didn't care what they wrote about, I just wanted to see their handwriting. I hung a bulletin board with quotations about handwriting and set up two old school desks with notebooks on them, trying my hardest to create a classroom atmosphere on a tiny budget and in the confines of the decrepit and largely-disused building where the exhibit was held.

The experiment worked pretty well. All through the show's opening I watched people stand in line to sit at one of the awkward little desks and answer one of the writing prompts I'd carefully written in a couple of cheap drugstore notebooks. A few weeks later when the show came down, I went and collected the books and got a big kick out of those stories—not just reading them, but looking at them too. Being able to see the hand a story was written in gave it another dimension, made it less perfect and, somehow, more precious.

I'm not the only one interested in the subject of handwriting right now. I've got a Google alert on it and it seems like once a week someone writes an article or think piece about it. I think the reason people are talking about it is that things are changing. The world is changing, and it's caused our own behavior to change. Of all the people who do written work of any kind, the vast majority now do it on a keyboard instead of paper. I believe that these kinds of changes aren't entirely good or entirely bad. I just find it interesting to look at them, and see how they affect our lives.

A short essay posted in the *New Yorker*'s books blog in August 2011 reported confidently that "cursive [is] no longer mandatory in most public schools," though anecdotally I've heard a variety of reports about penmanship in school. Some schools require it and some don't; some teachers like it, others think it's a waste of time. Still, there's no denying that learning and using cursive handwriting isn't considered as important as it once was. A *New York Times* article from April, 2011 reported on high school and college-age kids who don't really know how to write in cursive and—more worryingly (and actually kind of freaky, to me at least)—have a hard time reading it, too. A *Wall Street Journal* article published in October, 2010 discussed a link between writing by hand (not just cursive, but any kind of writing) and brain functioning. Apparently some scientists think that performing the actions involved in writing by hand helps us to imagine and remember them better than the action of hitting keys on a keyboard does. The article paraphrased a psychology professor as saying that "pictures of the brain have illustrated that sequential finger movements activated massive regions involved in thinking, language, and working memory—the system for temporarily storing and managing information." Hey hey Lynda Barry, whaddaya know?

I'm also interested in a certain fetishization of handwriting that has starting to take place in mainstream American culture. In 2011, a magazine called *Good* organized a thirty-day "live better" challenge and encouraged its readers to participate by answering the questions it posed on Facebook or Twitter. On one of the thirty days the editors asked: "How often do you write by hand?" Here are some of the answers they received and posted on their website:

Only on post-it notes and thank you cards.

Every day. I wish cursive writing wasn't such a dying art.

Every day, I journal.

I *love* to write letters—it makes people so happy and often surprises them and that is *good*!

Do whiteboards count? We have them all over the place at my office.

It's funny to think of using a stylus to make markings symbolic of language as an example of "living better," but I think I understand it. As digital becomes the default medium, people treat writing by hand as a hobby, a luxury, or even an art.

Some of the articles I've read report specifically on the decline of the use of cursive in favor of block printing, but when I talk about writing by hand I'm not referring to cursive writing exclusively. I don't care about whether or not people learn to write script in school, really. I'm just into seeing the scratches people make by hand—on paper, white board, bus stop walls, bathroom stalls. I get excited by personal stories and by people's attempts to communicate with each other. Glamorizing old shit just because it's old may be silly, but that doesn't mean I don't find it sad when people abandon things of real value just because a newer version has come along. Believing you have to choose one over the other is just more of that boring old false dichotomy: books vs. the Internet, digital vs. print. You don't have to choose. You can have both. I do.

A few years ago when I was poking around on ancestry.com, I found scans of several handwritten census reports from my grandparents' childhoods. All the information about the houses on these blocks and the people who lived in them was written in the beautiful and flowery but totally legible script of the person who had visited them there. In a row-house in an old Philadelphia neighborhood on the Delaware River, a census taker sat down in my great-grandparents' living room and took notes on who was there that year: my grandpop, age 7, his parents, a couple of relatives from Germany, two older sisters and an older brother and the littlest brother, Herbie, who was only 3 and would be dead two years later from scarlet fever. When I searched for this information I didn't expect to find a scan of the actual report, and watching those ornate, quirky markings load up and fill my computer screen was really moving. It felt sad to think of all those people who are dead and gone now, and the emotion was stirred in me largely because I was able to see evidence of that humanity in the census taker's handwriting. For just a moment, in my mind, they came back to bright life again.

There's something about standing on the edge of a changing era that makes us want to look more closely at the things we used to consider essential. There's a museum about 20 miles outside of Philadelphia called the Mercer Museum. It's housed in a tall cement "castle" built by a rich man named Henry Mercer in the 1870s, and it is a truly eccentric place. Mercer's idea was that the world was changing, and that many of the tools and methods that were the standard ways of making and doing things during his lifetime were soon to become obsolete. He made it his mission to collect them and put them on display in a museum, the true home of their near future—not to desperately try to keep the change from happening, but to record it. When you visit the museum, you walk along staircases that are the opposite of steep; they wind slowly around and go gently up the perimeter of the cylindrical building, and set into the walls for you to peer into are small rooms crammed with all this pre-industrial stuff. There are thousands of instruments for things like threshing, tin smithing, engraving, and leather working. A wooden whaleboat hangs from the ceiling. Up on the top floor, which feels like an attic but has a higher ceiling, is the bigger, creepier stuff: a horse-and-buggy hearse, a prisoner's block, a gallows. It's claustrophobic up there.

I studied linguistics in college, and one thing we were told again and again was that the written language is not the language. Our professors told us this repeatedly because we kept forgetting it, kept conflating the text we saw on the page with the language itself, when actually it is merely a representation of the real thing. Studying linguistics helped me learn to understand alphabets as an artifact, text as an object. I like finding shopping lists and other notes people have left behind in stores or dropped on the ground. I like knowing who a handwritten letter is from before I even see the person's name. I like it when a book I've checked out of the library is covered in marginalia, those personal notes people write to themselves (and maybe also to an accidental, occasional kind of audience, like putting graffiti on your own bathroom wall). I like that the software program I composed this essay in has an ink pot and quill as its icon. It's like the way a tiny picture of an old-fashioned phone, with its two round cups for talking into and listening out of, can be found on the "talk" button of a cell phone, which itself, of course, looks nothing like a "real" phone. Have you ever written with an ink and quill? I haven't. I've talked on those old phones, the ones with a handset and a cradle that are attached to the wall by a cord, but that was a long time ago now.

3.

Invisible Weaver

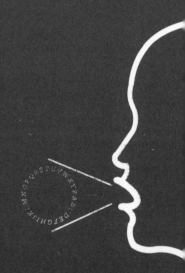

To look at me on any given day you may not be able to tell, but I am very particular about my clothes. Most of the stuff I wear is secondhand, even the newer, trendier clothes from Forever 21 or H&M, which I've most often found in a thrift store or at a yard sale, hanging from the branch of a tree on someone's front lawn. As approximately fifty percent of you know, the sizing of women's clothing can vary greatly, and it has changed over the years, which means that when you look at anything made before 1990 the real meaning of "size 4" or "size 14" is almost impossible to guess. Since this is how I shop, I have developed a good eye for what is likely to fit me. I usually ignore whatever the tag says and if I don't feel like trying something on, I'll just hold it out in front of me and squint. For a dollar or five, I'm willing to take the risk that a pair of pants or a sweater might not fit me, especially since I know I can alter it if I need to.

I've gotten pretty handy with the old sewing machine. I own one, a Brother XL 5600, that my mother gave me as a birthday gift a good few years before I was mature enough to be able to sit down and learn how to use it properly. I used to get so frustrated with it, taking forever to wind the bobbin and thread the needle and somehow always jamming it within the first minute of actually sewing. But over the years I've gotten more patient, and my need has grown. I am more interested in clothing now than I used to be, and my interest grew at about the same rate that my cheapness did. I have found that I can afford to have a large and varied wardrobe by doing small alterations to secondhand clothes myself, and by occasionally tracing patterns of my favorite pieces so that I can replace them with something similar after they've worn out. It's been worth it, taking the time to learn to operate the machine. These days the fabric is less apt to bunch and seize up under the needle; instead it glides through the machine like a warm knife through butter.

The fixes I've come up with are either messy concoctions of my own design—Crop-top? Sure! The scissors are in the kitchen!— or else very simple and common alterations, like taking up a hem. Since I'm not actually any good at this, the quality of my work varies. The first time I tried to turn baggy, high-waisted mom jeans into figure-hugging skinny jeans they came out wrong and ballooned at the hips like jodhpurs. Terrible. But I got the hang of it eventually, and so help me God I will never wear another pair of boot-cut pants for as long as I live.

One of the projects I'm proudest of is the hem I gave to a light green polyester skirt that I liked in every way except for its dowdy length. It's a lovely soft color and has a bit of comfy elastic at the waist, and its synthetic fabric never wrinkles. But it fell to calf-length and honestly looked dreadful on me, with my bone-white ankles poking out of the bottom. So I hacked about a foot and a half off the bottom of the skirt, turned the edge under, and went to work sewing it up until I saw that my machine was creating a very visible and unattractive hemline. Yipes! That wasn't how the skirt looked originally, I didn't think, but I had no idea why. I pulled the thread out with my seam ripper (the tiny, knife-sharp jimmy-jam that's shaped like a wishbone—such a useful little tool) and called my mom to ask her what I should do.

Oh, just make an invisible hem, she said.

Invisible! How magical that sounded. But how? Turns out it was as simple as slowing down and sewing it by hand, only putting the thread all the way through to the front every several stitches or so. I tried it and it worked. The stitches disappeared. When I wear the skirt now, you can't tell that it ever looked any different, that it wasn't just this way when I found it hanging in the musty one-dollar room of a thrift shop in south Jersey. It's not just shorter, it hangs better, and my little calves look way less pitiful now that my curvy behind is a featured player.

The phrase "invisible hem" has stayed with me. There's just something so awfully poetic about it. And it gets better. Though I don't often refer to the sewing instructions in them, I do own a small library of books on fashion and costumes. Paging through one of them recently, I learned that just as there is such a thing as an invisible hem, there is also a job called invisible weaver, also known as invisible mender. This refers to a tailor who can expertly repair a tear in an article of clothing, particularly in something that is hard to mend, like suiting fabric. The task is to make the clothes look like new, and if the mender is completely successful then we never even need to know he exists.

•　　•　　•

Each year the University of Pennsylvania hosts a series of public lectures on a theme, and one year the theme was "change." They scheduled a talk on "The Mysteries of Translation," and the speaker was Alastair Reid, a Scottish writer who is probably best known for his translations of poetry by Borges and Neruda from Spanish into English. The translation of poetry is a topic that interests me, so I put the lecture on my calendar and looked forward to it for weeks.

The talk was held in the cozy lecture hall in Penn's archeology museum, which happens to be one of my favorite places in the world. As kids, my parents took us there and my sister and I loved standing in the dusky wing of Ancient Egypt, staring at the mummies until we got a proper shiver. Years later I went to college at Penn, and I took a few anthropology courses that were held in the classrooms on the Museum's second floor. Sometimes I'd buy a small lunch at the cafeteria and eat it before class, sitting in the windowed dining room that was surrounded on either side by primordial-looking fern gardens. It felt like such a blessing to be there, I swear.

On the evening of the lecture I settled happily into my bouncy auditorium seat and plopped my bag into my lap. Alastair Reid came up to the podium and surprised me by being pretty old, but I realized that of course he'd have to be, if he'd been translating Borges and Neruda when those guys were writing back in the sixties. He told us that he lived for many years in Latin America, but he grew up speaking his native Scots at home and with his friends. Never in the classroom, though—they had to speak the dominant, "correct" English language there. He said that Scots developed out of a severe Calvinism, which he thinks is reflected in the language. For him, learning Spanish was an "opening up." "I had so much more fun in Spanish than I ever did in English," he said, which made me smile. We all smiled, I think. He said: "When you learn another language deeply you grow another self completely."

Reid knew Borges. They were friends. Neruda, who Reid also knew personally, once famously placed his hand on Reid's shoulder and asked him not to simply translate his poems, but to "improve" them. Is it necessary to know the poet whose work you're translating? I wouldn't have thought so, but maybe poetry has more to do with human connections than it ever did with theory or PhDs. In *The Wild Braid*, a book Stanley Kunitz made with a photographer just before he turned 100, he writes that to properly understand a poem you need to know where it came from: who wrote it, where that person lived, and what their life had been like until the point of writing it. The thing about translating a poem, when it comes down to it, is that you aren't just bringing it from one language into another. You have to write a new poem, one that gets inside the mind of the first one. "When you translate someone's work well," Reid said, giving us a proper shiver, "you become them."

Alastair Reid has lived an incredibly varied and itinerant life, one that seems enviable and impressive and kind of hard to believe to a homebody like me. In his memoirish collection of essays, *Whereabouts: Notes on Being a Foreigner*, he writes about the many, many homes of others that he has stayed in and visited throughout his life, even just within New York City, where he bounced around from apartment to apartment and had an office at the *New Yorker*, where he was a staff writer. In that book he uses the word translation in the most wonderful way, to describe the transformation he underwent simply by changing location. For a time he and his son owned and lived on a houseboat in London that was moored in Chelsea, and they made special arrangements with friends in other parts of that massive city to switch homes for a weekend now and again. (How have I never thought to try this? Let's all try it! We could have a dozen pied-à-terres!) Reid seems to have a special understanding for the objects in our lives, and although (or maybe because) he hasn't tended to settle into any one living space for long stretches, he appreciates the "extremely complex ... act of inhabiting and humanizing a house." I dearly wish I knew Alastair Reid, and that I could ask him to share his feelings on clothes, those dwellings and self-made identities we carry with us everywhere.

He seemed to enjoy himself up there that night, talking to us about language and art and the mind. As he spoke I thought about how unusually down to earth he seemed, how warm and honest and happy. And it struck me that his unpretentious personality shouldn't come as any surprise; I mean the job of translating someone else's work might be the ultimate in not drawing attention to yourself, like being a ghost writer. Or an invisible mender, if you will, who makes his work so perfect that he himself disappears.

I get a lot of pleasure out of thinking of this poet as a mender, and of my altered secondhand clothing like poems in translation, probably because I have such an abiding love for things that are old and new at the same time. Third-rate seamstresses and first-rate poets alike, we all change the things we touch when we imbue them with ourselves. However unimportant our little lives may be, however invisible we may sometimes feel, we create the world around us just by being in it.

The Bobo Way

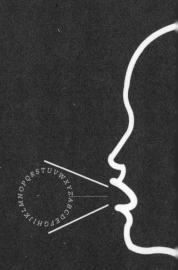

I grew up on the outskirts of Philadelphia and went to a Catholic high school in the section of the city known as the Northeast. It's an unsophisticated and much-maligned neighborhood made up of battered pizza places, row-houses sided in vinyl, and city buses that belch and lurch, but it's a sweet, safe place that I can best describe as cozy. I liked it there then and I like it there now, when I go back to visit. We girls—it was an all-girls' school—spoke with strong Philly accents, and we also had quirky things in our vernacular that I grew to feel ashamed of. Later still I grew to feel proud of them instead.

One word that I never registered as slang was bobo. That's what we called our sneakers, those cheap white canvas ones you could find at Woolworth's or Kmart, stacked up in a bin. Bobos. Bobos weren't great for gym because they were so flimsy and flat-footed, but everybody had a pair. They looked cute with jean shorts and if the mood struck, you could write on them with a pen or with that squeezable puffy paint and hope your mom wouldn't get mad. Most likely she wouldn't care though, cuz they were just your old bobos.

I still live a couple miles from my old high school; have lived here all this time. And one summer many years after I graduated, I worked at a nearby thrift store for one day a week. There was this beautiful girl named Annie who worked there too, in the women's clothes section; she was a singer and a musician and she had a really highly developed sense of personal style. I saw her wearing a flannel with a black leather jacket way before I saw any other girls doing it. Sometimes her black hair was styled close to her head and sometimes it was done in long bushy curls down her back. Anyway, she and I got to talking one day about her music and she told me she'd been working on recording some songs. I said, "Good for you, DIY! How do you do it?" And she said, with unnecessary embarrassment, "Oh, I'm just using a tape recorder. The bobo way."

Bobo! That word! I hadn't heard it in years. It used to mean cheap sneakers and now, I guess, it just means cheap. Boy did it make me happy to hear that.

Dear Friend

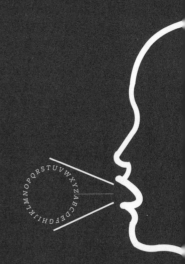

There was a time when I was really interested in reading about what America was like in 1911. This is because the house I grew up in was built in 1911, and I love that house, and its hundredth birthday was approaching. My mother still lives in the house, so I'm able to spend time there. And over the course of one summer, which felt slow and elongated by the heat, I fixated on trying to find out everything I could about the people who built it and what life would have been like for them.

I realize that 100 years isn't such a long time, but the hundred years of the twentieth century were unusually full, with lots of things getting invented and many others becoming obsolete. Daily life would have been rather different for those folks than it is today, and the details of that—what people wore, how they cooked dinner—seemed fascinating to me. I visited the local historic society, which is housed in the basement of the very small and charming branch library. Volunteers manage the newspaper clippings, school yearbooks, town records, and personal items (like scrapbooks and family photos) that comprise the collection. It's open to the public for a few hours every week; you don't have to make an appointment, you just have to be brave enough to walk down the stairs into the quiet, cramped space and be prepared to do your research at the same table where a handful of old people are also sitting, cutting obituaries out of the day's paper. Some of those volunteers are seasoned researchers who really enjoy the problem of finding something obscure. With the help of one woman I went poking through their filing cabinets and binders and was eventually able to look at handwritten blueprints of the block my family's house is on that were drawn up the year before it was built— which was weird, seeing a blank spot where the house should be—and the next year, when the house was built and had an address. The 100-year-old, careful architectural lettering looked Art Deco and special, though these papers were as ordinary as any town records.

The Johnson family built the house I grew up in and lived in it for the next sixty years. The parents eventually divorced, and one of the three boys studied to become a concert pianist, an ambition he didn't realize. He was the one I was able to learn the most about, the oldest of the three. In my mind he always wore a suit because the pictures I found of him were portraits taken at his high school graduation, but he probably did wear a suit every day anyway. One of his brothers grew up to marry a woman from Belfast whose uncles were shipbuilders on the Titanic. I learned all this from obituaries and yearbooks, piecing together half-reported facts like an amateur sleuth.

In my parents' dining room, on the floor underneath the table, is a small buzzer, which we poked with our toes during Thanksgiving dinner when we were kids. When the house was inhabited by its first owners, that button actually worked. It was wired to ring a bell outside of the maid's room, a tiny space on the third floor that my parents used as storage space. I guess if the poor girl was up there on her teensy cot trying to read a book, the Johnsons could summon her downstairs and tell her they needed more butter for their toast, or something. From reading school yearbooks and newspaper articles I learned that, beginning a couple years after they moved in, the Johnsons could walk up the street to see a movie at the brand new theater (called "the Auditorium"), which is still there and has recently been refurbished with its original fixtures. Back then, the musical soundtrack was provided by an organist who sat up at the front, near the screen.

I relished thinking about the people who had walked on our wood floors, hung their clothing in the same closets, and nursed dreams about their futures, the same way I did when I lived there. It further fascinated me to think of being "rich" all that long time ago, since in my family no one ever was. Getting a divorce at the turn of the last century sounded so decadent and sophisticated, I could hardly believe it. The majority of my family has always been Catholic, and in 1911 my ancestors, some of whom were Catholics of Irish and German extraction, lived in old, working-class neighborhoods in Philadelphia, where they worked as shopkeepers and delivery men. My great-great grandfather on my mother's side owned a slaughterhouse that was just a few blocks from where they lived. My father's father, who I never knew, was half Jewish, and as a kid in 1911—I've found census records for all of these people—he was living on a block in South Philly where the parents of nearly every household listed their language of origin as Yiddish. Growing up, whenever we made the corny joke of wishing the maid's bell still worked, my dad enjoyed reminding us that if we'd been in the house back then, we would have been the maids.

The house was wired for electricity when it was built, when electrified houses were still somewhat new. It also had gas lines for lighting lanterns that were fixed to the walls. On the blueprint for the house itself you can see the chute in the basement where coal was delivered, and the house was heated by burning the coal in a furnace down there. When I was growing up, our furnace was scary enough, the way it clicked on and rumbled to life by itself. The coal-burning one must have been the mother of all scary-basement furnaces.

I haven't been able to tell if the Johnsons had a telephone when their house was brand new. The historical society has some old phone books, but none from that year. I do know they would have sent a lot of mail. One of the nicest things about the year 1911 is that it was during the "golden age" of postcards, which lasted for about eight years. Back then it was common for there to be two mail deliveries a day, and people used the post to send practical messages that they needed to arrive in a hurry. Sending mail was also simply a popular pastime, and for a while there was a craze for collecting and sending pretty picture postcards. The simpler ones cost a penny, and the U.S. Postal Service estimates that, during this peak period, a billion postcards were sent through the mail each year.

I know all this because, years before I developed a dorky interest in the year 1911, I indulged a dorky interest in handwritten correspondence by bidding on a box of old postcards on eBay. When I won them they were mailed to me from someone's cigarette-smoky house, and I still have them all. They were originally written and sent during this golden era and most are from the same general part of the country I live in, only closer to the Midwest—Pennsylvania and Ohio—and the addresses are more rural than the Johnsons' / mine. Looking at the way they were addressed, it's touching and surprising to see what passes for enough information. Some of them only say the person's name and the names of their town and state: "Mrs. A.J. Whipple, Ashtabula Ohio." (The writer of that one asks Mrs. Whipple to meet her on the platform the next day, when she'll arrive on the

1:00 train.) Another card, also sent to an address in Ashtabula, was written by a kid named Ruth to her friend Grace. "I am going to school here in town now, am in eight[h] grade and have a man teacher."

Most of the cards are written in script, which is beautiful to look at but challenging to decipher. The lettering, much of it in pencil, has faded, some of the ink has bled, and on many of the cards the message is partly obscured by rubber stamps added by the post office. Almost all of the handwriting looks impossibly elaborate and sophisticated to our modern eyes, but the writers' differing personalities (some sophisticated, some not) shine through their words.

One message, which doesn't address its recipient by name, simply announces brightly, "Got my glasses alright. Feel just fine."

Others sound almost plaintive in their simplicity.

> Dear Friend—
>
> received your card. It was a little cold this morning.
>
> Good-by

My favorites are the ones with just enough detail to be evocative, and leave me wondering what the lives of the writer, and the recipient, were like.

> "Hello Pearle! You w/ your better 1/2 come to the dance Thursday Eve at Factory. I believe it will be warm enough so John won't freeze his feet."

Pearle had gotten a chatty card from a different woman just two weeks earlier, who talked about sleigh rides and the fine time she'd had at a party, and expressed her hope that they could get G.H. to take them into town on Saturday. Oh, how I wish I knew what Pearle looked like. It sounded like she knew how to enjoy herself, or at least had friends who did. I bet she had great hair.

Some of the postcards interest me because they provide details of life at the turn of the twentieth century:

"Dear Myrtle, Got home safely, canned yesterday, got 8 qts, a couple of pies, and had plenty to eat of the basket I brought. Pretty good, wasn't it."

"Dear Mother, I am at my sister's yet and am having a good time with lots of good, rich milk to drink."

(I saw a few examples on these postcards of yet being used to mean still. I think this is a regionalism, rather than an old-fashioned usage, but I'm not sure.)

Alva wrote to her sister Hazel: "I could not get you the Old Gray Bonnet they did not have more so I did not know what to get."

Others interest me because they wink with a certain intelligence and wit that the majority lack. ("Dear Jane: Am glad you think I have good taste. Arthur")

In general I like thinking about how, while the handwriting on these cards is lovely and the spelling is a bit better than the samples you'll find on the average page of Youtube comments, they aren't evidence of vastly superior literacy skills. They don't come from some idealized past when everyone was civilized and gracious, before life got ruined by TV and smart phones, or whatever. They come from the real past, where people varied, just as they do now, and plenty of them didn't need to know how to spell many words, and possibly didn't care much about it either. This is heartening to me.

I like thinking about the Johnsons sitting in the rooms of their house, writing postcards and letters like these at their desks, writing homework, writing lists. I did all those things there too. A letter can travel to a different location but it can also communicate across time. Anything you put down on paper could end up being a message to a person who hasn't been born yet, and who will read it long after you've died. The same could well be true of digital communication, but we don't yet know what the future of those messages will be. Right now, sitting at my desk writing this, the only thing I have to go on is a stack of yellowed pieces of paper, each covered in words that were meant to be read by one person, once, but have had a much longer and more interesting life than that.

6.

The Prick With The Stick

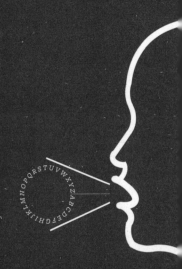

"I hear they're bringing back the floozy in the jacuzzi," my friend Rob said one day, out of the blue. We were sitting at the kitchen table in his rented house in Dublin, drinking tea.

"Sorry?"

"The hoo-er in the sewer," he said, trying to suppress a smile.

"I'm afraid I don't know what you're talking about."

"It's from the *Wake*," he said, meaning *Finnegans Wake*, the famous and famously obscure novel by James Joyce. One of the ones that no one's read but everyone—everyone in Ireland, anyway—refers to with the easy familiarity and fond disregard you'd use to talk about a crackpot cousin's get-rich-quick schemes.

"It's a statue of a woman in the bath, one of the characters from the book. They took it down a few years ago but they're putting it back up."

"I don't see why she has to have derogatory nicknames," I sniffed. "It's only because she's a woman."

He considered this for a second, then let the smile bloom. "Maybe, but you know what people call the statue of Joyce where he's leaning on his cane? The prick with the stick."

•　　•　　•

I'd moved to Dublin to attend a graduate program in modern English literature at University College Dublin—the same school, incidentally, that Joyce graduated from in 1903. Trinity, also located in Dublin, is the finer school with the fancier reputation. But since it was founded in 1592 as a Protestant-only institution, Joyce, as a Catholic, wasn't allowed by the Catholic Church to attend.

That's not the reason I went to UCD, naturally. I went there because I wanted to study literature and I wanted to live in Ireland—because after a weeklong visit there the year before, I knew it was a place I had to get back to. After I'd opened my acceptance letter and had stopped jumping up and down and throwing kisses to my cat, I went online to look for a place to live. On a real-estate website I found an ad for a room in a "worker's cottage," so called because it was one of many built in the mid-1800s by Guinness to house its employees. Could it have been more perfect? A little over a month later, I was on Philip's doorstep.

Philip was a portrait painter from Liverpool, a floppy-haired man in his forties who owned the house and rented out the warren-like back bedroom for extra income. It was a miniature place—I could walk from the front door to the little step out back where we hung our clothes to dry in six, maybe seven big strides. Our row of cottages was just down the road from a big, ugly housing project, which Philip warned me to avoid at night. The littler kids from the projects were sweet, though. A pack of them used to come down and bang on Philip's front window to ask if his cat could come out to play. This one boy Shane absolutely killed me. He was around seven, but little, with a long, solemn face and a textbook Dub accent. "I bet you're American, isn't it?" he asked me when he heard mine.

Philip and I got along pretty well—in a house of that size it was either get along or relocate—and for my birthday the next month he gave me *New Dubliners*, a collection of short stories by contemporary Dublin writers published in honor of the Bloomsday centenary.

When I got to Clare Boylan's hilarious story about the antics of a few rollicking neighborhood kids, I heard Shane's voice on every page. ("'The sisters was bigger than us,'" her main character Francie says. "'Even though they were still stupid and scaldy, there was older guys making eyes at them.'") I was thrilled and moved to find myself living in a story—and a good one at that.

•   •   •

Three times a week I took the notoriously unreliable number 17 bus from my neighborhood to campus. At the first meeting of our Theories of Modern Literature class, we broke up into groups of four to prepare a presentation on an avant garde poem that went on for several pages and, for many, many lines, repeated the mystifying "ribble bobble pimlico." My group spent the 15 minutes developing plausible theories on the poem's meaning while I made wisecracks and got sweaty armpits at the prospect of contributing something useful. That might have been my first clue that I wasn't a match for the program. I did have a good time at the pub afterwards, though.

My professors were insightful, deadpan, easy-going. Every Wednesday evening after lecture they trooped us down to the faculty lounge for complimentary drinks. It was the lecture part I wasn't so keen on. I couldn't get a handle on the convoluted constructs we were supposed to shoehorn into the poems and novels we read. The Marxist philosopher and literary critic Georg Lukacs liked to say things like, "Abstract potentiality belongs wholly to the realm of subjectivity; whereas concrete potentiality is concerned with the dialectic between the individual's subjectivity and objective reality."

I suppose I'm revealing my provincialism here, but I didn't see what that sort of thing had to do with the beautiful poetry and prose we were reading—by Eliot, Pound, Joyce—or with any other piece of writing I've ever loved. My instructors, and a few of my classmates, could deconstruct this literature and the culture that had produced it in one dazzling academic flourish—and fair play to them, as they say in Ireland. I just didn't get it.

By the time I decided to drop out of the program a couple months later, I considered Dublin a second home. People there had a certain everyday connection to their literary culture that was exciting in its ordinariness. A friend of mine from class, who dressed all in black and owned every piece of paraphernalia used to promote the movie *Corpse Bride*, was the daughter of a couple who owned a small bookshop in the countryside. Her apartment was filled with little stacks of books like ancient druid burial mounds, and she had a photo of Terry Pratchett on her cell phone.

Of course, there was Rob too, whom I'd been dating for a few months and had sort of fallen in love with. He and I met in a pub on my birthday, and before we'd even gone out on our first proper date, we bumped into each other again at the Irish Writers' Centre, where a friend of mine from class was having a book launch party. Late that evening we had a long...very long, very sweet kiss on the stairs out front, and I was done for.

Once I'd dropped out of school, I had no compelling reason to stay in Philip's dumpy neighborhood, so I crammed some clothes into my backpack and bought a bus ticket to the other side of the country. I cycled solo around the hauntingly beautiful Aran Islands; I peered over the edge of the dizzying, dazzling Cliffs of Moher. Out of school and on the road, I finally had time to go where I wanted and read what I liked.

For my journey, my goth friend gave me a somber John McGahern novel, overstock from her parents' store. Another friend lent me a book of poems by Eavan Boland that I read on the bus, green fields and stone walls rolling by me outside the window. In Derry, I went on the piss with a rowdy bunch of Northern Irish drinkers, some of whom really knew their way around a bookstore. The next morning, my head sore and stomach quivering, I opened the little notebook I carried with me everywhere and was touched to find a recommended-Irish-reading list one of them had written for me.

Back in gray, damp Dublin, I crashed with friends and read and wrote. I was tired and dirty from not having a place to live, but I tried not to care what I looked—or smelled—like and just took it in. Drifting through the city I walked past the full-color statue of Oscar Wilde lounging on a rock, past the loony street poet peddling his books with a sign that advertised "lovely poems, no hard words." I nosed around Hodges Figgis, the beautiful bookstore whose name conjures up characters from Harry Potter. I sneaked into Trinity's library and looked up William Trevor books; I sat in the stacks and cried at the end of *The Day We Got Drunk On Cake*, wiping my face with my ratty sweater.

I read more in those few months than in any other few months from the rest of my life—as a student, a book reviewer, a lifelong lover of words.

I stayed at Rob's place sometimes, too, where I drank gallons of tea and literally ran through the kitchen on my way to the bathroom every morning because the floor was as cold as an ice rink. He and I were supposed to spend my last week in Ireland together, traveling outside the city for a B&B getaway, but our relationship had unraveled by then. On the evening of its final sputtering death throes, we sniped at each other and cried, and by the end of it I was too worn out to leave and find another place to stay. Instead we lay there on his bed, sad and defeated, him paging halfheartedly through the Murakami novel I'd just finished and me hiding in his copy of John Banville's *The Sea*, which, with its droll asides and descriptions like poetry, helped me keep my wits on that unhappy day. I didn't give it back.

In the morning I left his little house for the last time and took the bus downtown. I spent hours that day in bookstores—the bright and shiny Hodges Figgis, where I got my own copy of *The Sea*, and a cluttered used bookstore that was also a post office. I left there with a few gems, including a battered copy of *The Kilkenny Magazine*, Autumn-Winter 1961. Truth be told, I bought it because of the fantastic hand-drawn Guinness ad on its inside cover. A line of sad-sounding books sat on one shelf: *Les Miserables*, *Bleak House*, *Anatomy of Melancholy*. On the shelf below—and next to an empty pint glass—were the comically chipper titles *Present Laughter* and *The Merry Wives of Windsor*. The ad's tagline: "Life is brighter after Guinness."

The next day, the day before my flight home, I decided to do a few touristy things I'd put off, which included a visit to a museum exhibit of Irish literature I'd read about in the paper. When I got there, I realized it was the same place where I'd toasted my friend's book and shared a glass of wine with Rob, whom I hadn't yet begun to love, or unlove. I lit a cigarette, sat down on the cold stone steps, and opened *The Sea*. It was the last piece of beauty I stole from that place, but not the only one. Not by far.

On The
Word Slut

I used to be so metal. I loved all the bands: Queensrÿche, Faster Pussycat, L.A. Guns, and Poison, who I always thought were cheesy because their songs were too catchy; Motley Crue, Skid Row, and Extreme, with guitarist Nuno Bettencourt, he with the shining black hair and the most memorable name in the business. I was into Metallica and Megadeth too, but the guys in those bands were angrier and not as good to look at, although Kirk Hammet always struck me as sort of sexy.

I was the only girl in my sixth grade class who liked these bands; it was, like so many things in my life would turn out to be, an entirely solitary pursuit. This music spoke to me completely. It was loud and exciting—sometimes fun and sexy, other times dark and angry—and finding it felt like bringing back to life a part of myself that had been languishing because I could no longer run wild through the neighborhood and climb trees like a boy. I asked for the tapes and CDs as gifts and, when I didn't get them, used whatever pocket money I had to buy them myself. And even though I owned a copy of GN'R *Lies* on tape, I still sat in the kitchen every evening calling Eagle 106, the local terrible rock station, over and over again until I got through so I could request the song "Patience." "I'll try to get to it, okay hon?" the DJ would always say, not unkindly, before hanging up, and he usually did. Probably lots of other kids had also called to request it, but when it came on the radio it felt personal, like the other half of a conversation.

I studied *Metal Edge* and *Circus* magazines, looking for interviews. I wheedled and begged to be allowed to stay up late once a week to watch the *Headbanger's Ball* on MTV, which didn't even start until midnight. Alone in our basement rec room, I smoked my mom's stolen cigarette butts, True Menthol 100s. It's gross to remember now, but sometimes she'd stub one out before it was really finished, and I could always get them to light enough to suck a few more minty drags out of them. I'd sit there "smoking" and dreaming I was on the battered *Headbanger's Ball* couch, with Tommy Lee being interviewed by Rikki Rachtman. Maybe I was in the band, maybe I was a girlfriend, maybe I worked for the show and everyone could tell I was cool enough to just hang out. It was hard to come up with a story that fit me into this scenario, actually, because this was such a male world.

But there were women in the scene. Some of them, not many, but a few, were in bands, and they were badass. Sexy, too. Lita Ford looked like a pirate wench and a biker all rolled into one, and there was no denying her power. She sang a ballad with Ozzy for christsakes! But most of the other metal chicks were just, you know, hot. They weren't in the bands, they just were in the videos—standing around in short skirts and high heels or pulling off their tops at Def Leppard concerts. The status of these women was a little confusing. They seemed to be integral to the success of the thing—the videos, the concerts would be pointless without them—yet clearly they were secondary to the men making the music. No one ever uttered the word slut, but it hung there like a fart.

The individual women were more or less interchangeable: In the "California Girls" video David Lee Roth worshiped them, but there was an endless line of them, which made it clear that to be a slut was to be one of many. Then again, in the "Hot for Teacher" video, the teacher-stripper was the star. She was powerful and subversive and no one could take their eyes off her. ("I don't feel tardy!" Say it out loud—it sounds like "tarty.") I learned about all this in the magazines, too. In the back of *Metal Edge*, every month, were several pages of band t-shirts and other merch you could order, and there were always about ten dozen Samantha Fox posters.

Oh, Samantha Fox. You were so slutty! And so clearly a cause for celebration, a person everyone who read the magazine was meant to admire. She had teased, bleached hair and wore crop-tops, cut-offs, ripped-up t shirts that showed her midriff, leather jackets, leather bodysuits, and those 80s bikini bottoms that came up really high and were shaped like a V. Often she was topless and covering her breasts with her crossed arms. Samantha Fox's idea of being a woman didn't seem to have anything to do with who I was or what my body looked like, but I didn't dislike her for what she was doing. In fact I was a little thrilled and turned on by it, and fascinated, too, by the sort of shabby power she seemed to have harnessed. This, of course, is the secret heart of the word slut. I knew without being told that slutty was a bad thing to be, except ... clearly, it wasn't entirely bad. Samantha Fox was pretty and famous, desirable and cool. Weren't those all good things?

Yeah, the word slut. What does it even mean? I thought I knew what it meant back then. I knew that you could "tell" that a girl was slutty just to look at her, and that clothing had something to do with it. I knew there was a difference between nice girls and girls who wanted everyone to know that they were sexy, which was not nice of them. Lipstick, lip liner, foundation makeup: slutty. Eye makeup, long nails, chewing gum. Ankle boots. High heels. A purse when you were too young to carry one. Tall bangs, crunchy with hairspray. So many things could mark you as a slut; it was a minefield.

I also understood that being slutty had something to do with where you were from, what kind of family you had. If you were from a certain neighborhood, if your parents seemed a little trashy, if you got head lice in third grade or had an older brother who was a mechanic or a sister who was on the pill, it would be that much easier for you to become a slut. Smoking could make you slut. Getting bad grades, too. It was all sort of the same thing. It was important to be pretty, extremely important, but it was equally important to be polite and prim and more or less invisible.

And to be honest, that year I was wishing I was invisible. I had just turned twelve, and the world was beginning to respond to me in a new way—the same way it probably responded to you, if you had a girl's body when you were twelve. I was about as skinny as a kid could be and hadn't yet developed breasts or hips that amounted to much, but somehow I had changed, and men, adult men, saw it even before even I did. And they stared. When I went out in public, to the mall with my mom, their eyes went to me—dorky, little-kid me, who nobody had cared about only a year before. They did it even though I wore old dungarees and t-shirts, or the pleated skirts or modest dresses that had been deemed appropriate for someone my age. It didn't happen all the time but it happened often, when it had never happened before. Their attention scared and confused me and since I didn't dress "like a slut" it had the weird effect of making me think they could sense something about me that was more innate than that, something I couldn't control. I was bad, this was obvious to others, and therefore I had no choice but to absorb their attention while pretending not to notice it. What else could you do?

I buried those shameful feelings for a long time, and had to work to keep them stuffed down pretty much every day, when men would stare at me or yell things from cars, and when bosses who were married and as old as my dad tried to trick me into being alone with them. I tried to own my appearance, and used clothes to deflect male attention or twist it into something new. When I was in my twenties I learned to consider every outfit a costume, even when the theme was something as mundane as "doing the food shopping." On any given day I have dressed like a hippie, a hipster, an office lady, an old lady, or a grown-up tomboy. I have stacked my arm with bangle bracelets, worn ugly eyeglasses, wrapped thick soft espadrille laces up my legs, clomped around in motorcycle boots, carried my mom's old purses, and worn my dad's old jackets. I don't usually "do" my hair and I'm not good at applying makeup, but I can wear the hell out of a pencil skirt and some heels. I like the way that dressing up can make me feel like I'm wearing a costume, like I'm in drag as a woman even though I am a woman. Sometimes I like that, doing drag, and sometimes I don't.

•   •   •

If the year I turned twelve—the year strange men began making me feel scared and embarrassed but sometimes powerful too, the year I got my first period and I was in love with Joe Tedesca, who everyone said kept a condom in his wallet and who had no interest in me at all—if that was the year when the idea of slut took shape in my mind, then many years later, in 2011, when a cop told a group of college students in Toronto who had assembled for a talk on campus safety that the women could avoid sexual assault by not dressing too slutty, well, that sort of felt like the year of the slut too.

Those women in Toronto organized a protest march, and I silently cheered them from my apartment in Philadelphia. When I heard through the grapevine that people were organizing a so-called Slut Walk in my city, too, I wanted to go. This felt like my fight. Thinking about it, I had a powerful image of myself taking the subway to the march like an aging riot grrrl, with the word SLUT written on my skin in marker or lipstick.

But ... and I want to laugh just writing this ... I didn't know what to wear. I could dress ironically, symbolically, like a slut, but how? Should I wear fishnets? I used to own some but I looked in my underwear drawer and they didn't seem to be there. High heels? I have tons of those, but I don't consider any of them slutty. I was starting to hurt my own feelings thinking of my clothing this way. As the date of the Walk drew closer, the old, old discomfort started to creep in. What if there was something wrong with my clothing and I didn't know it? I felt a shiver of cold dread thinking of people snickering at the idea of me at a Slut Walk: "Well she'll have plenty of clothes to choose from." I was equally, truly, just as afraid that I'd hear the opposite, that I was too dowdy, too old or too dorky to look slutty even if I tried. The question of what to wear to the Slut Walk was threatening my equilibrium, my feminism even.

And then I thought, Fuck this. Why was I having this trouble? There are clothes that I like and clothes I don't like, things I would wear and things I wouldn't, but that old question—What makes a girl a slut?—it wasn't interesting anymore.

In the end I wore what I would wear on any trip into town. I put on my comfortable stylish new knee-length Vivienne Tam skirt in slate-colored linen ($12 on sale at T.J. Maxx!); a 90s-era tank top from the thrift store that has a print of red, blue, green, black, and yellow doodles; and these weird pink flip-flops that have an extra couple of straps on them, so they look sort of like sandals. When it came down to it, I found I couldn't bring myself to write the word SLUT on my body or my clothes, and not even on my sign, on which I wrote instead, in neat black block letters, DON'T PARTICIPATE IN GIRL HATE. It was a slogan I'd once seen on a patch that was sewn onto a stranger's backpack, and I liked it, mostly because it rhymes.

The morning of the Slut Walk I took the train into the city and walked toward the small park where I'd planned to meet my friend Raquel. She—along with dozens of other women and girls and some guys—was already there, wearing a red tank top and being her usual generous self, giving out the leftover poster board that she'd bought that morning to make her own sign.

When the time came we all walked for several blocks through center city Philly, right down the middle of the street. Some of the sidewalks were lined with people taking our pictures or cheering us on. I felt publicly powerful, looked at but not leered at. Appreciated. I held my sign over my head as I walked and repeated the chants the leaders of the march started over megaphones. We all did. We were the Slut Walkers but none of us was a slut, we were just girls and women who looked like regular people because we were regular people. Some of us, somewhere in our past, have been raped. Most of us, myself included, have been cornered, threatened, groped, abused, ridiculed, stared at, yelled at, or stalked. All of us, I bet, have been called slut, bitch, or cunt by men and women we know, and by strangers on the street. We've all been trained to think—and probably have thought, at times—that these things happened to us because of how we were dressed or what we did or didn't do, but this isn't true. We have to learn to recognize these insidious, invisible messages that surround us and we have to be honest with ourselves about the way we participate in perpetuating them. We have to stop thinking of ourselves and other women in this way. Every time we call someone a hateful name we corrode their dignity and make it easier for someone else, someone who would like to hurt them a lot worse than that, to go ahead and do it and feel like it's okay.

You know what's weird about Samantha Fox? I looked her up online when I was writing this piece and it turns out she was in a band. She was a singer who sold more than 20 million records. I forgot that somehow.

I am an unmarried woman in my thirties and I have slept with men I loved, men I didn't love, and once with a man I didn't even know and never saw again after that night. When I was younger and much smaller-breasted, I never wore a bra, and for a few glorious years I had a pair of Diesel jeans that I packed my round ass into so tight I could hardly sit down. By some people's standards I'm a prude—fussy about who I'll give my attention to, never laughing at a dirty joke. By other definitions I suppose I might qualify as a slut. But I'm not afraid that someone will use that word against me anymore. The fact that, in this weird world, I could be either a prude or a slut doesn't confuse me anymore. I know who I am and it's neither of those things, because none of us is either of those things.

In the end, when I tried to decide how to dress for the Slut Walk, I went as myself.

8.

Another Word For Lonely

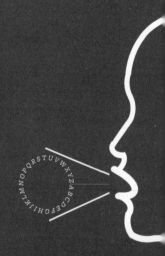

This girl I know through doing zines told me she was planning to start a zine and call it *Saudade*. I wished her luck and asked her: What does the name mean? It's a Portuguese word that has no equivalent in English, she said, but she could kind of translate: It means a sense of longing or yearning, most likely for something that is lost and probably can't be found again. Ah, I thought. There may not be an English word for that but I know what it feels like, yes I do.

I went on to read more about the word and found that yes, it is thought to be untranslatable into English. But there is a similar word in Finnish: kaiho. If saudade is a romantic restlessness, a "vague and constant desire for something that does not and probably cannot exist ... a turning towards the past or towards the future" then kaiho, it seems, is something more like loneliness, "a state of involuntary solitude in which the subject feels incompleteness and yearns for something unattainable or extremely difficult and tedious to attain." Something about this word touched me, even more than saudade did—I think it was the chilly hollowness of the way it sounds—and I wrote a poem about it that day. The slanted language of poetry, plus the gift of this new word—the secret door it opened into a language and culture I know nothing about—this linguistic twistiness gave me a way to talk about something I find hard to feel, let alone discuss; a loneliness, a sense that I'm on my way home but I'm not there yet, a feeling that follows me everywhere, bobbing along and tugging at me like a bright balloon someone tied to my wrist so as not to lose me at some cheerful outing a long time ago.

When you first learn about something you see it everywhere. One afternoon around this same time, I walked over to the small library in my neighborhood to have a look around. This library is not housed in a romantic old building but is one of those squat, black, one-story deals with tinted windows that looked modern in the sixties and just looks kind of ugly now. But I love it there. So many trees surround the building, you can sit in one of the armchairs and look out the window as you read and feel like you're in a treehouse. On this occasion I hadn't come looking for anything in particular, so I walked slowly up and down the aisles, gazing at the books' spines, when I spotted one in the travel section that looked different from the others. Sure enough, it wasn't a travel guide at all, but a reflection on the Italian city of Trieste by the Welsh travel writer Jan Morris. Right there on the second page of her book, Jan taught me a beautiful word of Welsh Gaelic: hiraeth. This word, like saudade, means a kind of yearning; it too has no direct translation into English, allegedly. As far as I can tell it means a kind of homesickness, a longing for an idealized home. That one gets even closer to the feeling I have: nostalgia, but for something you don't remember. I get surprised, almost assaulted by this feeling sometimes, don't you? I get it during the summer, deep in the heart of the season when it's really hot and still; there's still half the season left to go but the quality of the light has begun to change, to ease up just a little, so that I can feel the autumn hiding inside of it. I'll step outside and a pang of longing will slice my insides, and I'll know I want something but I won't know what it is. It's as if there's a house I want to live in, if only I could find it. It's a specific house, one I can almost picture, but somehow I know I've never been there before. Maybe it's a house from a dream. I long for it, yes, I'm homesick, nostalgic for a place I've never been. I can't possibly be the only English speaker to ever feel this way, yet we don't have a word to describe the feeling in English. Why?

Sometimes I'm guilty of getting too many ideas from books instead of life, and that's not ideal for language, since real language is the thing that's spoken, not the thing that's written down. I needed to ask some real live people with blood running through their veins and brains to tell me what they knew about these words. So I wrote to my friend Janine, who's English, and asked if she knew any Welsh speakers I could talk to about hiraeth, and she did. She introduced me to her friend Owain, who said:

"I will gladly dive into this conversation with all the lust and vigour of a fat horse that finds itself locked in a cupboard. Let me thrash about.

Yes.

Hiraeth is one of those sort-of-untranslatable words, linguistically. The word Hiraeth may render itself very specifically to the Welsh language but the emotion/sensation it conveys is that general/human sense of 'yearning' ... a longing for the place that you 'belong,' geographically or emotionally.

In a Welsh context it embraces a sense of sweet, aching melancholy. It can also tip-toe into rampant (almost operatic) sentimentality—in that way that consumes you when you find yourself separated from something that you know is intrinsic to your being. Our legends and poetry are full of hearts torn apart by the sensations of Hiraeth. It can be an intense and all-consuming festival of tears or a sharp jab in the heart that stops you in your tracks.

Of course, if you're not careful you find yourself wallowing in a rather maudlin swamp of loss and separation sensations, and without The Wellington Boots of Rationality you might become a little bit wet.

It's all very emotional.

That's about as close and concise (!) as I can steer with these clumsy hands. If only I had a head that worked ... I can only hope I haven't broken anything."

Well I couldn't have asked for anything better than that.

•   •   •

The only language I know reasonably well besides English is German, and that's only from high school and my own plodding attempts to speak to people on a visit there and read the text on European websites about music or fashion. I've always felt a lot of affection for the language. It has a no-nonsense mentality that I find touching and takes its efficiency to an almost comic level. German will often and easily produce a many-lettered word that's actually three or even four words pushed together, without altering any of them, because it's the simplest way to describe the object or concept. Never mind that the word, in print or in your mouth, is a bit much. It's exactly accurate and that's what matters.

Not long ago I spent an evening sitting in my apartment listening to this band I like, Einstürzende Neubauten. I listened carefully to the words to see how much of the German lyrics I could understand, and when it came out of my speakers I translated the phrase immer noch to myself. It means still, as in I'm still here, but the literal translation is odd and sounds almost like poetry. "Always already," that's what it means. Trying to conceptualize this seemed to make my mind a little more elastic, like I was making room for more stuff.

The next morning I rooted around on the Internet for explanations of the phrase and to my surprise I found it everywhere. Turns out always-already is, well, already a thing, first used by German philosophers and now discussed in philosophy generally. One example of always-already is the idea that the language you speak shapes the way you think. The argument says that you have always already known your language of origin, so your perception of all things is necessarily filtered through these words. This idea is interesting and I think it's probably mostly true. But what about kaiho, hiraeth, saudade? I'd felt those feelings long before I ever had words for them.

As it turns out, German has a word for this feeling too, and it's somewhat better known by English speakers than those others. Sehnsucht. It means "longing, yearning, ardent desire; pining, nostalgia." C.S. Lewis wrote about Sehnsucht, and to him it was a spiritual thing, this "inconsolable longing" for "we know now what." In his book The Problem of Pain he wrote:

"All the things that have deeply possessed your soul have been but hints of it—tantalizing glimpses, promises never quite fulfilled, echoes that died away just as they caught your ear. But if it should really become manifest—if there ever came an echo that did not die away but swelled into the sound itself— you would know it. Beyond all possibility of doubt you would say 'Here at last is the thing I was made for.' We cannot tell each other about it. It is the secret signature of each soul, the incommunicable and unappeasable want . . . which we shall still desire on our deathbeds . . . Your place in heaven will seem to be made for you and you alone, because you were made for it— made for it stitch by stitch as a glove is made for a hand."

I really couldn't have asked for anything better than that.

•   •   •

In all my thinking about these foreign words I forgot to talk about the English one, nostalgia. But that word, it's got an interesting history too. It was coined by a Swiss doctor in the seventeenth century to mean "severe homesickness," and it was considered a physical illness. (All other words that end in -algia are medical terms. It comes from the Greek word for pain.) Apparently Swiss soldiers were experiencing the symptoms of nostalgia at this time because they were away from home, and being so displaced was making them sick. A Harvard professor named Svetlana Boym has written about this extensively, having spent years studying the manifestations and ideas behind nostalgia. She writes that one doctor in the seventeenth century called it a "hypochondria of the heart, that thrives on its symptoms." Remedies during this time included purging, leaches, and opium. Today, writes the professor, it's a nearly universal feeling and no one looks for a cure.

I take her meaning, but I do. Look for a cure, that is. I am nostalgic, almost painfully so, and often for things I don't remember. I love kitsch for its sadness, its former beauty made ludicrous by time. I love obsolete, forgotten objects. I love ink wells and frilly aprons and heavy typewriters with dusty ribbons that might have some life in them yet. I love these things purely, and without a sense of irony, although I used to dress up my feelings as irony—to hide their tenderness, I think. To protect it. I keep collecting this old stuff at flea markets and yard sales, and filling my home with them soothes my longing temporarily, but in the end only stokes it higher. It thrives on its symptoms.

The thing is, those words—saudade, kaiho, hiraeth, sehnsucht— are all defined with the same disclaimer, that they have no equivalent in English. When I was first reading and thinking about them I accepted this at face value; it was one of the things that drew me to them in the first place. It's fascinating to think about how culture and language shape the way we see the world, and words that can't be translated seem to highlight this, as though the speaker of one language might be able to see something that would be invisible to a speaker of a language without a word for it.

But you know, I'm not so sure I think this is true anymore. I think these words may only seem to have no translation because the feelings are so hard to grasp, so hard to put into words to begin with.

Sometimes the closest you can get is a poem.

Kaiho

The last best word I learned before today was mirabile visu—okay,

two words—Latin for "wondrous to behold." After learning

it I saw wonder everywhere, I beheld it: hopping brown sparrows and

the tender new blacktop outside on my street, freshly rolled.

But today there's this: kaiho, Finnish for something we haven't

named in English, "an involuntary solitude" like yearning

with a pang of knowing that the yearned-for thing can never

be. In my mind kaiho rhymes with I go and I want to

but there's all this work to do, birds to envy and streets to stalk,

the windows of the houses flashing sunlight so I can't see in.

9.

Completely Human Nonsense

A Russian woman named Nadia who lives in St. Petersburg once contacted me online, saying she wanted to buy some of the zines I had for sale but she didn't have a credit card. Of course we don't use the same currency so I couldn't invite her to just send me a couple bucks in the mail, which prompted her to mention things like Western Union. The money exchange started to feel confusing and pointless so I suggested a trade, hoping she was a zine maker herself, maybe, and would know what I meant. She didn't make zines but it turned out that she liked the idea of a trade. "Oh yes, I see, I send you a gift," she said. I put the zines in the mail to her and forgot about it.

But then, several weeks later, my gift arrived, tall and thin and sturdy when I tapped on the brown paper wrapping. On the outside were special-looking stamps and writing in a strange alphabet that I can transliterate, but can't read. (I know how it sounds, but not what it means.) Inside the wrapping I found a beautiful hardbound book of children's poetry, illustrated in watercolors and written in Russian. Nadia explained to me, in simple, halting English, that this gift was more than just a pretty book, that children's poetry was an important way for poets of the Soviet era to write with some kind of honesty, however coded and secretive, without fear of imprisonment.

In early Soviet times, censorship caused many artists to stop producing work, and many others were put in prison. In later times laws were passed that interpreted political dissent as mental illness, which made it legal for people who publicly disagreed with the government to be locked in mental institutions for indefinite periods of time. In *Words Will Break Cement*, Masha Gessen's book about Moscow-based activists Pussy Riot, Gessen writes that in all societies, public rhetoric is based on some form of a lie, but in the "really scary" ones every word uttered in public is used to mean its opposite. It becomes so dangerous to tell the truth that the word—the world—gets turned inside out. Nadezhda Mandelstam, a Soviet-era writer who was married to the poet Osip Mandelstam (who died while being transported to the Siberian labor camp where he'd been exiled), published two memoirs about the couple's lives under the Stalinist regime. In one of them, *Hope Against Hope*, she wrote that as the social climate grew more oppressive, everyone began to seem like a potential threat. "People started to avoid each other... Only the children continued to babble their completely human nonsense." In many ways, the language children use, with its imaginary creatures and unfailingly honest silliness, was the perfect one for poets, too.

Nadia told me that these children's poems, with their subversive double meanings, are dear to Russian people today, but I don't know a lot about life in the early days of the USSR so I don't know how much got through back in the twenties and thirties, when the Soviet state was brand new and still growing steam. Did parents read books to their little kids at night and chuckle, understanding the rebellion inside them? Or were the poems a secret even from their readers, simply a way for the artists to publish something, anything, and keep from going crazy?

Nadia and I stayed in touch, and in my next letter I told her about the only zine I own in Russian, which is (I think) about the punk scene in Minsk. I offered to send it to her since she'd be able to enjoy it in a way that I can't, but it turned out she already had it. She wasn't very interested in its contents, she said, but at least she could read the thing. About the coincidence of our both owning the zine—*Zoom Doom* it was called, a tiny publication that neither of us could really make use of—she wrote, "I can say the world is big puzzle," which I understood to mean that everything will fit together in the end, but for the time being, it's hard to see how.

10

Blood &
Thunder

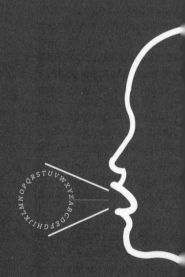

"Well they look like a couple of rounders to me."

My mom was peering out the window to spy on the neighbors when she said this to me. She thought she was giving me some useful information about the people milling around on her neighbor's front porch, waiting to be let in, but the truth is, as so often happened when I was growing up—and sometimes, like on this occasion, still does—I had no idea what she was talking about.

My mother has been speaking her own quirky language for as long as I can remember. One day when I was about 8 my sister and I were playing out back when the girls next door started acting snotty. Especially Margot, who was my age. She taunted us from behind the hedge that separated our yards, saying that if we touched their tree her father would sue us, which he could do because he was a lawyer. Liz and I hurried inside with this news, but mom was unimpressed.

"Tom the cat's a lawyer," she said, scoffing. Liz and I looked at each other and started to cackle. Tom the cat? Like the cartoon? Mom was so weird sometimes. But while the picture the expression conjured was hard to make sense of, the disregard beneath it came through loud and clear.

All my life my mother has drawn from a seemingly inexhaustible supply of mordant expressions that use silly words and preposterous imagery. When Liz and I pestered her for too long she told us to go chase ourselves. A showoff was a blaster, and showing off—or putting on airs—was definitely bad. (Although if someone was about to do something special, like get new living room furniture, she'd say, "You won't know yourself!" and that was good.) People who had an attitude about something had their asses up; my aunt Maggy has had her ass up for about 20 years. And if you were making something up, you were talking through your hat.

"If you think I sound funny," my mom told me and my sister once, "you should have known my grandmother."

I never met my great-grandmother, but I've been told that by the time she died she was speaking almost entirely in Anglo-Irish idiom. For instance, her only son Joseph died when he was only 28, of tuberculosis, which he got in the war. But my grandmom, his sister, always said that the real reason he didn't recover, the reason his lungs wouldn't dry out even after 18 months in an Arizona sanitarium, was because he was wild. Handsome and red-haired with the temperament to match, Joseph had already blown through one marriage by the time he left for the war. Through the grapevine the family found out that the girl went on to marry someone else, a man who'd done jail time for breaking into a neighborhood house. The new husband's name is lost to history, but everyone remembers that my great-grandmother just referred to him as "that second-story man."

I know that some of these sayings aren't Irish in origin, but most of the people I'm talking about are. Wherever these sayings came from, my sister and I grew up hearing things around our house that we never heard anywhere else. It was a secret language, in a way, and not just because no one else talked quite the way my mother did. You had to listen close to hear the meaning in the music. And it wasn't just the words I liked, but the stories they told, whole lives unfurling behind them.

When I asked her, my mom explained that rounders are ne'er-do-wells, drinkers, lazy bums. "People you'd see going 'round to the bars a lot," she added, after a moment's thought. My mother and her mother had a whole passel of expressions for drinking. It seemed like someone was always being criticized for getting a toot on or a snootful or having a few belts too many. Back in the twenties, my grandmother's family ran a taproom in an old working-class neighborhood in Philadelphia where her family has lived since practically always. She said it was a bright little room that did a good business, but whenever she pitched in, wiping up tables and sweeping the floor, she would see the men who sat with their elbows on the bar all day, getting into the occasional fight and eventually being dragged home by their sad, angry wives (or worse, their young sons). It was there that my grandmom learned something useful: too much drink can get you into trouble. It's a lesson I had to learn myself, well past the time I should have known it already.

When I was in my twenties and working at a newspaper, I fell in love with one of the other writers there, this great-looking guy named Jimmy with a gorgeous head of dark hair and skin so white it looked like his fine, keen features had been carved out of marble. He was from Brooklyn and his pop was a fireman but he was a poet, and he had a sexy tattoo. Not a trendy one, but an old-school Celtic cross festooned with shamrocks that blazed across his biceps in merchant-marine blue. He was the kind of guy I would have tripped over ten times a day if my family had never left the old neighborhood, but in my sheltered suburban experience he was the epitome of old-fashioned masculinity.

But things with Jimmy went bad quickly. Are you surprised? There was always so much drinking and chaos, so much apologizing and romancing the morning after. Eventually I understood that the drinking and the passion were bound together in some way I could never untangle, and that I couldn't stay with him without losing myself. After we broke up, and the flowers and late-night phone calls had stopped coming, my mom felt comfortable telling me what she'd thought of him all along.

"With men like that," she said, "it's nothing but blood and thunder."

I just looked at her. The meaning of that one was clear—poetic, even—but I remember feeling amazed that her storehouse of expressions still hadn't run out. I've since looked into it and found that some of her turns of phrase, like second-story man, are not all that unusual. There's even a play by that name; I think it's by Upton Sinclair. But if you ask my mother where her sayings come from, she'll tell you it was just something her mother used to say. And in a way that's true too.

The Morans, and her family on the other side too, came to Philadelphia from Ireland around 150 years ago, at a time when more than half the people in Ireland still spoke Irish. The English that Irish people spoke back then, and to a certain extent speak now, was touched by that language, which you can hear in its inflections and turns of phrase. When those immigrants came to America, their culture, like all immigrants', was a private one that thrived in the home. It was in that rarefied place that they used their language to turn the indignities of everyday life into something like poetry. Those old turns of phrase became a kind of family lexicon that has lasted all this time, surviving even a move to the suburbs, where the man next door is a lawyer.

It's the language of survival, to be sure. But more than anything, my family's way of talking about the world told me what kind of people they were—cool in the way that only people who have to earn it can be, snarky before the word snark was invented. My mother grew up fresh-faced and safe outside the city, her long blond hair shining. But she never lost that city attitude—never walked around in someone else's shoes, as Jimmy used to say. I like to think she's passed some of that powerful sass down to me through the words she used.

For all her clichés, my mother doesn't care for upbeat platitudes. Her favorite expressions are short and not especially sweet. "You could hang for that long" was her stock response to any complaint about a some short-lived torture, like math class or Mass. "Like it or lump it!" she'd trumpet merrily on her way out of the room, ending all discussion. Before she delivers one of these gems she twists her thin Irish mouth into a smirk, and there's never any mistaking the wisdom in her words.

"Your mother's much smarter than I am," my dad told me once when I was a kid, as though that was some kind of secret. I wonder if he ever told her that. Somehow I bet he didn't. From the way she talked, anybody could see she already knew.

11.

On The Words Hussy, Harlot, and Madam

In college, I took up the kind of major that made even the most bookish types say, "What are you gonna do with that?"

I started out figuring I'd be an English major. I'd wanted to be a writer for as long as I could remember, and my academic experience to that point had indicated that English was what I was best at. English everything: grammar, literature, even penmanship. The other subjects I was less enthusiastic about. I'd flailed around in math classes my whole life, trying to make sense of things I simply didn't have the imagination for. "What do you mean, the number goes into another number?" I remember demanding of my dad about five minutes before I sent the textbook sailing across the kitchen.

No, I didn't seem to be built for anything but English. But the English courses I enrolled in my freshman year of college took a backseat to one I selected sort of by accident. The course book, to my great delight, informed me that Linguistics 102 would fulfill the same requirements as calculus. I had blundered my way through baby calculus during my senior year of high school. Honestly, if I tried right now, I don't think could come up with a single word to explain what calculus actually is. While most of my friends signed up for calc to cross the "formal reasoning and analysis" category off of their list of required courses, I knew I wouldn't be able to hack it, so I signed up for this linguistics thing instead. Back then, the word linguistics wasn't quite as mainstream as it seems to be now. When I enrolled in the class I didn't really know what it was. I just knew it had to do with language, so I figured that meant I couldn't not like it.

On our first day of class, our teacher, a grad-student T.A., told us to think of the subject as the architecture of language, the structures that held it together and made it work. It thrilled me to think of a thing like language having underpinnings, let alone ones we could take apart—to peek under the hood of the way we communicate with each other and see the mechanics of it all. It was different from any sort of mental exercise I'd ever encountered, almost philosophical in the way that it showed me a part of myself that was as essential and natural as breathing and eating but was actually made up largely of cultural constructs so, in another sense, totally arbitrary and contrived.

Our class met twice a week in a half-basement classroom in the late afternoon. It was winter term—I still remember that, all these years later, because I can picture the light in the room, the way it dimmed while we sat there and turned into night by the time we left for home. Our T.A.—I wish I could remember her name—had us read a book called *The Language Instinct* by Stephen Pinker. Pinker is a linguist who has published a number of other books since then and is pretty famous now; he's a bona fide academic, a cognitive scientist and linguistics professor at M.I.T. and Harvard, but he often writes on the mind, the brain, and evolution for places like the *New York Times*. But *The Language Instinct* was his first mainstream, not-scholarly book, and it had come out that year. People were very excited about it. Among its many attributes was the way it made Noam Chomsky's work so easy for non-academic readers to understand. Pinker wrote a fair amount about Chomsky's notion of nativism, the idea that the capacity for language is "hard-wired" into our brains, that as little children we are like sponges soaking up the language around us and have a natural ability—an instinct, if you will—not only to use the language but to improve on it. An example of such an improvement is the first generation of children born to speakers of a pidgin language, which is a cobbled-together compromise between two or more languages that have come into contact, usually because of colonialism, commercial trade, or sometimes slavery. The pidgin is much simpler than any natural language and has hardly any grammar structure. But the children born to the speakers of that pidgin give it a grammar, without even trying. Simply by learning to speak they make the language more robust, more real. We're made for making language, apparently, because without it we will die.

As evolutionary science has progressed, the basis of the nativism argument has come into question a bit. But that's not really the point I'm trying to make. What I want to tell you is how much this idea turned me on. I had always enjoyed telling stories, and writing them down, "being a writer," had been part of my personal identity for as long as I could remember. But here was this guy saying that my very ability to tell a story was integral to my humanity and not very unique at all, which made me feel closer to everyone, part of the human community that was ancient and primitive, inventive and forward-looking, all at once. We have different ways of expressing and showing it, but down deep, the book seemed to say that we are all the same. It put me in my place in the nicest of ways.

Up until this point, I'd only really thought about the things we can make with words: the books, poetry, and songs that meant so much to me. But learning to think about what the words themselves were made of, well, that was like a stick of dynamite blowing up inside my head. It felt that big, that explosive, and it made room for tons of new ideas to hatch. If you wanted, as a linguist, you could go even smaller, look not just at individual words and their histories, but at the components of those words, the individual sounds that comprised them, and even the way we articulate those sounds with our mouths and the way we hear them with our ears and brains. The physics of phonetics mapped beautiful mountain ranges across our primordial, nineties-era computer screens. Who says science isn't art?

Sitting in that classroom, though, in our little introductory course, we did learn a bit about individual words and their histories. And for me, this is where things got a little weird. Our sweet, passionate T.A. wanted to make a point about the way our use of language reflects the values of our society, so she taught us the etymology of a few words of English that sounded old-fashioned but were nonetheless kind of embarrassing to hear in a classroom: hussy, harlot, and madam.

Let's take a look at those words right now, shall we?

hussy n.1530, mistress of a household, housewife; ... In some areas the meaning changed to any woman or girl, and by 1650 applied to a woman or girl who shows casual or improper behavior (as in bold hussy); by the 1800s hussy acquired a generally derogatory meaning.

harlot n. Probably before 1200 heorlot vagabond or itinerant jester, later harlotte prostitute

madam n. probably before 1300 madame, borrowed from Old French ma dame, my lady

These three words all have two things in common. They are all gendered terms of abuse, and they are all words that began with a different, neutral (and in the case of harlot, also gender-neutral) meaning. Our teacher chose these examples to teach us about the semantic phenomenon of narrowing and degenerating word meanings, and also to make a point about woman-hate, which you can't help but find every-damn-where. Narrowing refers to words that initially described a superordinate category (all women or girls) come to represent only a subordinate one ("improper" women and girls), and degeneration refers to a word taking on a negative connotation over time. Few people still use the word madam as a polite term of address; these days it pretty much just means the head lady in a house of prostitution. The reason narrowing and degeneration happen in a language has nothing whatsoever to do with the words themselves, of course, but with the feeling underneath them that keeps rising up. We look down on women, so words that are used to refer to them disproportionately change their meanings over time to become either sexualized or insulting or both. Incredible the way we human beings can shrink our own world. The word *narrowing* just seems so apt.

In an essay for the *Historical Thesaurus of the OED*, authors Marc Alexander and Kate Wild describe how to use the OED's searchable thesaurus and explain some of the crappier cultural lessons we can learn from this etymological research. "We can compare the meanings and connotations of these slang terms for males ... with female terms... This is an illuminating way of exploring historical sexism expressed in English. Even a brief survey of the mini-definitions given in the Thesaurus browser shows the high number of words with 'derogatory' or 'contemptuous' in their meaning." Alexander and Wild go on to make another observation about sexism as it has been cemented in the English language by pointing out "the existence of a subsection of woman called 'as a means of sexual gratification.' This, needless to say, has no male equivalent."

Over the years, the thing about studying linguistics that has mattered to me the most is my idea that language is a kind of blend of instinct and intention, nature and nurture. Language isn't exactly a living thing, like a tree; it's a made thing, like a chair, but not just like that, because a chair can't change over time, seemingly on its own. Language acts like an organism but it's more like art, something we made for our own use and enjoyment, and for that reason it can only reflect the values of the people who invented it. Remembering this is key to surviving in this world. You most likely weren't born the thing people have told you you are; in fact, you might not be that thing at all.

But if people made up bigotry then people must be capable of stamping it out. Right?

All these years after my first linguistics class, this is what I remember best: The simple outrage my T.A. expressed on behalf of all the people who have been put down or insulted by their fellow folks at the level of the language that we speak, an atomic level, you might say. But remember, atoms aren't the smallest things. We can always dig a little deeper, look more closely, figure out where we went wrong.

12.

The Literal Worst

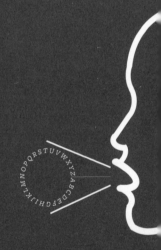

At the end of every year, a few magazines publish lists of the "worst" and most annoying new words. Sometimes the winners are goofy-sounding neologisms that were coined, usually by some magazine editor, to describe new objects or ideas, and sometimes they're smug little zeitgeisty terms like foodie and mancave (looking at you again, magazines). Sometimes the hated words are innocent, ordinary ones that for some reason started to be over-applied, running rampant in everyday speech. (The adjective "amazing" comes to mind.) When these lists are released online, people go nuts in the comments section, keen to chime in with their least favorite words, and I always feel left out because I expect to feel passionate about this subject too, but I don't. I mean, I am passionate about words. I love good writing—honestly, there are books that have saved my life, and that is no exaggeration—and the flipside of needing good writing is the disgust I can feel for writing that is false, lazy, or pandering. I hate it. I do. But somehow I can't find it in myself to hate the actual words.

Atlantic Monthly's winner for the worst word of 2012 was literally. People are angry about the way that word gets misused, like when someone says, "I literally died when I saw him yesterday." My feeling is that the people who use the word this way are probably being ironic. If they are, to be honest, I find that pretty funny. If they're not, then they must not know what the word literally means. So what? I'm sure I couldn't tell you what most of the symbols on the periodic table stand for at this point in my life, just to give you one example of all the many things I don't know. There are plenty of folks who do know what all the symbols on the periodic table stand for and they may well think my quality of life is diminished by not knowing it, and I guess it might be, but it doesn't feel that way. You can't know everything. I'm not too worried about it.

The thing is, language is flexible. It's made to grow, and it's natural for it to change. New words get made up to fill some need, and if they continue to be useful they'll stick around for a while. Also, word meanings narrow, expand, and otherwise change, and sometimes the usages that seem incorrect, the things that upset everybody so much, are merely changes in progress.

It reminds me of a conversation I had back when I was in college. I'd met a friend for dinner one night, and since I was studying linguistics and she was genuinely interested in the subject, Allison announced that she had two questions for me, both language-related and topical.

The first was about "ebonics." Ebonics was everywhere that year and Bill Labov, a professor of mine, was one of the experts in the field. He'd done groundbreaking work in the sixties on African American Vernacular English (AAVE), studying its differences from Standard English and showing how usages like ain't and the dropped -s in verbs for the third-person singular ("she go to school"), which a lot of people—including some of the Black folks who use them—dismiss as mere bad English, were just as grammatically functional as their counterparts in the standard language. Some linguists consider AAVE to be different enough from Standard English that it qualifies as a distinct dialect, making the Black Americans who switch back and forth between the two dialects diglossic. That's not as extreme a switch as bilingual speakers get used to making, but it is significant. Throughout that year I'd heard Bill interviewed on the radio and elsewhere, and everyone wanted to know whether ebonics was a real language or not. He'd had a hell of a time trying to explain the difference between this loaded political term that didn't have much linguistic meaning and how languages actually function. I tried to say the same things to Allison and I'm not sure I succeeded.

Her other question was about the word *chocoholic*, which she found embarrassing. This one I was excited to bloviate about because I'd taken an etymology class that year, where we learned that English, compared to other languages, is very productive. That means that it lends itself nicely to making new words by combining existing ones or by using abstractions, like the one that allows us to form chocoholic from alcoholic. This flexibility is one reason English has lasted so long, and through so many collisions with other languages. But Allison didn't care that much about how the words were made—she just wanted to know if I thought chocoholic sounded stupid, too.

And you know, I really didn't. I can't say I use the word myself, but it made me happy to think of it and it still does. I remember sitting there with her in the cheapest Chinese restaurant near campus, its humid air and clanking dishes from the kitchen making us feel cozy and safe. I remember smiling about it, about our big sprawling messy clever language—so old, so new.

13.

Heavenly Bodies

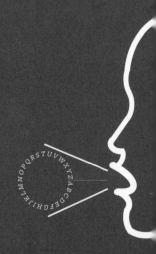

I got braces put on my teeth when I was in the eighth grade and didn't get them off until two years later. I didn't like having them, I guess. For those two years I refused to smile for school pictures because I didn't want to show my teeth; it bothered me that much, at least. But honestly I didn't care much about it. I didn't feel like kids in movies always seem to, mortified about how they'll never get a date. I didn't want a date, I wanted to stare at the album art inside my Ultramega OK CD and pretend that Chris Cornell, shirtless and screaming and gripping the mic, was my boyfriend. The boys I knew in real life just didn't interest me that much.

Once a month I left school during my lunch period and went to the dentist's office to get the braces tightened, a procedure that made me think of torturers twisting the screws on the rack, pulling my body in directions it wasn't meant to go. It hurt so much it made me drool like a dog. My only reliable memory of algebra is of sitting in the warm drowsy classroom after the appointment, each tooth throbbing like it had its own tiny heart.

But the dental hygienist lady who did the tightening was lovely. Her name was Soheila and she had long eyelashes and fat black curls, and she smelled like makeup. Looking back I can see I had a crush on her, but at the time all I knew is my scalp tingled when she fixed the paper bib around my neck or patted me, her hand in its tight glove, plastic-smooth, like Barbie's. When I first met her and she told me her name, she spelled it, smiling. She was always smiling. She told me that her name was Persian but that Persia isn't a country anymore, and this information astounded me, the idea that you could be from a place that no longer exists. Obviously this woman was pure magic.

I looked up the name Soheila just now and learned that it's the Farsi word for star.

14.

To Name Something Is To Own It

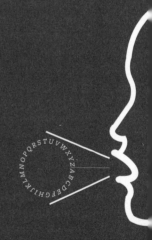

I visited San Francisco with my boyfriend, Joe, not too long ago. We were there so that I could participate in a reading series at the main branch of the city's beautiful public library, built a hundred years ago and rebuilt, in a massive modernization in chrome, in the late 1980s. We arrived the day before, just to be on the safe side, and settled into our rented apartment in a modest and quiet residential neighborhood that was mostly Asian— Chinese and Japanese. We were two blocks from the ocean and a ten-minute walk from the San Francisco Zoo, and since we had a whole day to kill before the reading, and since I was kind of nervous about doing it, we decided to go to the zoo.

I don't think I'd been to a zoo for more than twenty years. Maybe close to thirty. We went when we were very little kids, I guess, to the Philadelphia Zoo, but I don't even really have my own memories of that. When I think of "the zoo," I think about my mother's stories of taking my little sister's class there when she was in the eighth grade, and how annoyingly rambunctious the boys were, and how Michael Donahue climbed a fence and reached over to try to pull feathers out of a peacock's tail. He nearly got one but my mom caught him in time.

This zoo was different from the zoo of my imagination. It was a bright, breezy September day, with that clear-eyed California sunshine that shows you everything like an X-ray, even while it's pretending to be all laid-back and gentle. We went on a weekday, so it wasn't noisy and hectic, only a few families and here and there a mother pushing a baby stroller. There were no cotton candy vendors, which was the other thing I guess I remembered about the zoo: cotton candy. This was a more grown-up place than I expected it to be.

Joe and I stood for quite a while and watched a giraffe, who was new to the zoo, get to know her new herd-mates. She was in her own pen, separate from the others, but she kept bowing her long neck down over the fence to let one of the baby giraffes nuzzle her. When she got nervous she'd dance backward like a horse in slow motion. We saw some rhinos standing there being boring, the same color and shape and, seemingly, texture as the tan rocks around them. We saw a giant anteater and heard a guy say "His tongue is hella long!" and his girlfriend say "Don't say hella." We even saw some peacocks.

And then, booming and echoey, we heard something like a person's voice exploding over a loudspeaker, like the sound of the state fair from a distance. But it wasn't a person, we didn't think. We stopped and looked at each other.

"It's a bear," Joe said. "Or ... I don't know. It's really loud! Let's go see."

We followed the sound down a path lined with lush jungle growth, and it popped us out in front of the building marked "big cats." So it was a big cat making that noise. We walked gingerly into the building, which was empty in the center and ringed with cages behind glass enclosures.

In one of the cages, a beautiful tiger was roaring. It was hard to believe how loud his voice was, and he kept on doing it. Not in a ferocious way, exactly—he sounded more agitated than outraged and he kept busting out these short moans of complaint, one after the other.

The cat was huge. He moved just like my housecat companion, Trixie, who is now dearly departed but at one time was a lithe and muscular animal. His massive shoulders rolled forward with each languorous step. He was a male Sumatran tiger, a rare and endangered subspecies of only 400 living in the wild. His stripes, glossy and black, tapered into points at their ends and looked like they had been applied with a calligraphy brush. This tiger was the most beautiful and terrifying thing I have ever seen, and I didn't want to look away. After a few minutes he slumped down onto his side to chill, posing with his front paws in front of him like a sphinx, like Trixie. I started to cry.

I cry in this really embarrassing way every time I (a) hear sacred music played, live or in recording, or (b) see huge majestic animals that are predisposed to kill me, in real life or on TV. It's awkward but I can't help it. I just stood there, silent, staring at this massive animal with tears running down my face. I guess this is what is known as awe, a response to great beauty that is a combination of genuine fear and a kind of tenderness, a softening. If no one else had been there I think I would have fallen to my knees.

A small crowd of people gathered in front of the cage. The tiger was still carrying on. As he yelled he walked in a straight line through as many cages as he could until he reached a locked door, then turned around and paced back. A zookeeper in a trim green uniform came out from a door underneath the cages and walked across the enclosure, in front of the glass, to talk to us. She explained that the tiger had mated with a female and produced a cub, which he had never seen before today. By their nature, tigers are solitary, so this male tiger has been kept separate from the mother and baby. In the wild, if he encountered his own cub, he would kill it. Today, though, he'd been able to spot them both through a few layers of glass, and it had him all riled up. You could tell by the way the zookeeper looked at him that she had a personal relationship with the tiger, and likewise, he watched her with interest as she moved.

"Lar-ry," she chided, looking at him over her shoulder as if to say, "This guy, what are ya gonna do!?"

Jesus Christ. The tiger's name was Larry. Immediately the balloon of feeling that had filled my chest let out a little air. I'd always heard the idea that "to name something is to own it," and I thought I understood what was meant by that but could never really feel it. Looking at the tiger behind bars, I felt it for the first time. Even for a person, Larry is a sort of goofy name: A permanent nickname, seemingly owned only by middle-aged men who are somehow insubstantial and unthreatening. This animal that was never meant to have a name, had been given one that sounded like a joke.

I watched the wonderful tiger watching me, monitoring the feeling inside myself, which was decidedly quieter than it had been a moment ago. I felt less afraid right then, but sadder.

15.

What Do You Do?

Last summer I went to a street fair. I didn't much feel like being there. It was Memorial Day, a mild afternoon in early summer, and the party was taking place in a rapidly gentrifying area of the city, a neighborhood I've been to a number of times before. It lies very close to one of the roughest and most miserable parts of Philadelphia, a "bad" neighborhood that rivals every bad neighborhood in this country.

When I got off the bus I walked in the wrong direction and knew it immediately, without having to look at the street numbers. In neighborhoods like that, none of the buildings are marked anyway. Half of them are empty industrial buildings and the rest are empty lots with nothing there or houses, some of them inhabited, some not. As I walked I tried to take it all in but even in the most desolate areas there is so much everything, it's hard to know where to look. Weedy yards and patchy concrete and blank window holes with no glass in them like dead eyes; blasted-out blocks laid out in front of me like I could encounter anyone if I kept going, like in a dream where who knows what could happen next. I've had so many dreams like that. The only recurring nightmare I've ever had is of trying to cross a huge city alone at dusk with night coming quickly, looking out at the ruined, gothic terrain in front of me and not knowing which way to go.

Whenever I'm in neighborhoods dominated by crime I stand out in a way that makes me feel embarrassed, sorry, implicated, and afraid. Apparently, most people who look like me only go to places like that to buy drugs, which means that when I appear there, I am immediately pulled up into the life of the place. Cars slow to a roll beside me, and dealers on the corner leer and smirk. On this occasion, when I realized my mistake, I crossed the street and turned back and as I went, I nearly stepped on a dead cat on the sidewalk, and forced myself to stifle a scream.

It didn't take me long to find where I was going, once I'd turned myself around. I watched the neighborhood change block by block, become more lively, more leafy. Eventually I saw a fucking ivy-covered brick house. I hated the young white people with expensive haircuts who had started to come crawling out of every car and cafe, and I hated myself for looking just like them. By the time I turned onto the street blocked off with wooden horses and folding chairs, I was sweaty and pissed off and already tired. I grew up in and around this city, and having watched it change in different ways I can't decide which hurts me more: The squalor that has ruined schools, families, people's lives, or the smug newcomers from upstate wherever who squat in those places—literally or figuratively—and, for themselves anyway, make them safer.

I wandered through the party till I found my friend's table. People had set up stalls to sell things they'd made, and there was a rockabilly couple firing up burgers on a grill. My friend was selling the buttons she makes with feminist slogans on them, and her small table—I think it was her kitchen table— looked cheerful and inviting. As I got closer I was dismayed to see a jarringly beautiful girl standing there, talking to Rebecca. And she wasn't just beautiful, she was *correct*. Like normal, you know? She seemed out of place at this dirty-punk event, but was clearly the superior one as far as the larger culture was concerned. Her long hair was colored just the right shade of blonde, and you could tell that even her roots were supposed to show the way they did. I tried to be friendly but I could only handle smiling in her general direction, because looking directly at her was bumming me out. No, I did not want to be at this street fair at all. I went and bought a hot dog from the chick with a giant chest piece.

No one at the fair was familiar to me so eventually, grudgingly, I drifted back to Rebecca's table and stood there mopping up the relish on my blue plastic plate with the butt of my hot dog. She introduced me to her pretty friend and the girl seemed alright, actually. We all got to talking and this young woman, whose name was Annette, told me she was an artist, but she expressed frustration at having to define the sort of artist she was. I could relate to that, the embarrassing feeling that can come with having to define yourself neatly for a stranger.

"You know, I think it's an American thing," I said, trying to act like a decent human being. I told her how I'd lived in Ireland for a little while, where I figured out pretty quickly that it was considered bad manners to ask a stranger "what they did."

The several months I spent in Dublin, I wasn't so much a smug, squatting newcomer as a listless, overgrown kid whose family had come apart after her father died. I did try, though, in my messy way, to make that place a home. There was no language barrier for me to get over—not really—but the Irish do have a way of using English that's pretty different from what we Americans do. I only spent a year or so there, not long enough to even scratch the surface of another culture, but I did learn a few things about the people there, and about myself, when I saw the places where my culture bumped up against theirs.

When I met people out at the pub, or on the cramped little street where I rented a room, I quickly learned that "What do you do?" wasn't quite the thing to say. No one got angry about it, but they would look away in discomfort, even the ones who—it later turned out—had "good" jobs. Professions and specialties that would have been boast-worthy where I come from—software engineer, medievalist—were mumbled about with obvious embarrassment. Moreover, no one ever asked me what I "did," even though my accent gave me away as a foreigner, so my reason for being there would have made for an obvious item of polite conversation. I guess in Ireland, jobs are thought to be a boring topic of conversation, or possibly it's considered rude to talk about yourself at all, whereas we Americans are taught from an early age the value of presenting yourself with confidence.

Back in Ireland for my master's program in literature, I was amazed to see how difficult it was for my classmates, all of whom were Irish except for me and one other American woman, to speak up in class. One student, a sort of retro riot grrl who knitted lumpy "jumpers" during lectures, was so uncomfortable giving a presentation to our class of ten or eleven people that her cheeks and neck flushed a deep shade of purple that I'd never seen before on uninjured skin. I remember feeling worried that she would faint.

But back in the present in America, Annette seemed to get what I was saying, and I felt myself relaxing around her. She said: "What do you do, it's sort of a greeting, isn't it, more than anything else?"

She told me that she'd lived in Nepal for a couple of years (of *course* she did), and that on a long hike through the mountains she learned to greet strangers with a phrase that means "Have you had rice today?", which is a standard greeting in that part of the world. Rice is a staple food in Asia, and whether or not a person has had enough to eat seems a fair gauge of their happiness in any country. When I first got to Ireland I shook people's hands and said "Nice to meet you! What do you do!" but it didn't work. But as Annette suggested, I hadn't really meant anything by it. It was kind of just my way of saying, "Hello. I'm interested in you. Have you had rice today?"

It's a bad idea to read too much into one tiny piece of information about a culture you're otherwise ignorant of. Still, it's interesting. Most people in Ireland don't ask each other what they do because they don't care. I found that folks there valued other people, socially, I mean, for their warmth, their "realness," and their intelligence, and your level of intelligence is measured not by your profession but by your powers of conversation, your ability to toss a teasing joke back at the person who'd teased you first. It's probably not coincidental, either, that the people in a country that has long dealt with a high incidence of poverty and deprivation haven't learned to expect to get their only sense of identity from a job.

The area of Dublin where I lived was a cramped neighborhood not far from the city center, which is bustling but also small and cozy. Every place in Ireland felt cozy to me because the cloud-white sky was so low; in a weird way it felt like being inside all the time, except that I could never get warm. To get to the center of town I could either take a swift, silent tram car called the Luas, which is Irish for speed—a Luas stop was located directly across the road from our squat row of cottages—or walk the two miles up the road. I did both, often.

I Googled the stop's name just now to see if I could find any photos to stoke my still-warm memories of the place. (Like embers they'll still break apart and flare up a little, from time to time.) My search returned a news article on a "bottle attack" that took place at the stop earlier this year. A young man was viciously beaten with a broken bottle and left lying there to die.

(I couldn't find any follow-up news reports to find out whether he survived.) This is the kind of physical violence that exists in Ireland—no guns to speak of, and only occasionally knives. It's mostly fists and rocks and it isn't often random, the way it can be here.

I felt at home in Dublin in many ways, more at home than I have ever felt in the country where I'm from. Here was an entire country full of Catholic people, which is to say, people who used to be Catholic, which in the peculiar way of growing up Catholic means Catholic forever and ever in some way you just can't shake. Even after you reject it, it's a thing you keep on being. The haunted, weary knowledge of this is in the air there, and every person I met who eventually became a friend embodied this intoxicating combination of beat-downness and fiery resistance, a charming and pissy sort of rebellion for its own cantankerous sake. The people I got close to all seemed to feel the way I've always felt—dogged by sadness, but getting by anyway—though feeling this way has only ever made me lonely here at home. Finding myself in this place, realizing that I might fit in there, felt like such a relief, I can't tell you.

The guy who was beaten at the Luas stop was well known at the mansions up the street, the article said. Mansions is the improbable name for housing estates in the UK and Ireland, the grim, brutalist buildings constructed for use as government-funded housing. When I first moved in, Philip, the English guy whose cottage it was, told me to be careful walking past the mansions because one time kids there had winged flattened tin cans at him as he walked past.

Still, I rarely felt afraid there. At bars and on the street I did encounter some anti-American hostility ("I fuckin' hate Americans" a yuppie wearing a pink dress shirt once spat at me in an upscale pub), but I didn't often worry that I'd get attacked or mugged. Maybe I should have, but I didn't. I felt like I'd found a second home, an extended family, a Catholic grade school the size of a country, and it was an awfully comfortable way to feel.

It wasn't my home, but much of the warmth I felt from that place came out of the mouths of the people who wanted me to feel welcome there. One of my friends from grad school called me "cuz" when he saw me, short for cousin, as in cousin from across the pond. *Hey cuz.* I dated a Dublin native for much of my time there who still, after months, managed to surprise me with his charming turn of phrase. One night when we were due to meet up, he sent a message to my phone: "What's the scandal?" I thought he must have heard about something I hadn't, since the only thing happening around me that I could see was people drinking and laughing, the usual, nothing scandalous at all. He explained it to me later: It's just a turn of phrase. You know, like What's going on, what's the story. He had a twinkle in his eye when he told me this. His eyes often shone with humor, though he rarely smiled. Everything was a joke with them, which meant of course that nothing was, it could all turn deadly serious on a dime and someone would end up in a fist fight, or in tears. I liked these people and felt like one of them, but their home isn't my home, and eventually I had to leave.

But what does it really mean to have a home? Do you get to decide where you fit in, or is that decided for you by the accident of your birth? Do people who aren't poor ever have the right to live in places where the people are poor, or is it always slumming it, always some kind of despicable voyeurism? I honestly don't know. In my provincial way I have resented the privileged people who move into these old Philadelphia neighborhoods, believing, if only emotionally, that they have no right to be there. But I don't really have the answers to these questions, and nobody asked me anyway. Who gets to decide who belongs at the party?

In a way, I guess, the whole world belongs to all of us. I wasn't from Ireland and what's-her-name certainly has no claim on Nepal, but there we were, for a time. Outsiders, but we learned to talk the talk. In a world where the idea of home is constantly shifting whether we want it to or not, it's important to learn the best way to say hello, I'm interested in you, and to be sure we say it often.

16

Who Gives a Fuck About an Oxford Comma?

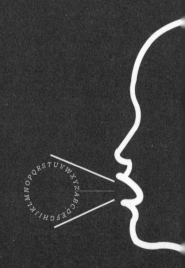

There is a thing that annoys me, and that thing is nerd culture. I am not talking about socially awkward, single-minded weirdos who love what they love and are oblivious to everything else. Those are real nerds. I like people like that. But all over the internet there are not-nerds, conventionally attractive and fairly with-it people who want to tell you that they are nerdy even though they are not. I know you're familiar with the phenomenon I'm referring to because it's everywhere. The tide turned some years ago, and it became stylish to dress like a Poindexter from the '60s. It became stylish. *Doing a thing that is stylish does not make you a nerd.*

But whatever. This is just a petty grievance of mine. Wear whatever kind of glasses you like, that's your business. The real problem about this attitude is the divisiveness it creates. One egregious example of this, in my view, is the "debate" that's been raging about the Oxford comma. Oh Lord, I feel so tired thinking about the Oxford comma thing, I can barely muster the energy to tell you about it. But don't worry everybody, I will. I'll tell you.

The expression, Oxford comma, refers to the last comma in a list of things, which is also called a serial comma. "I must remember to pack my toothbrush, denim jacket, and pleated pants." The comma before the word "and" is the Oxford comma. Deciding whether or not to use it is usually a stylistic choice, which means that—outside of the times that you must use one to avoid confusion—you may use it if you like the way it looks or sounds, but you don't have to. It got its name because the style manual put out by Oxford University Press recommends using it.

A few months ago, I started seeing a pissy back-and-forth about this on tumblr, the social networking platform I find myself on the most. Actually, there was no real back-and-forth—it was mostly a pile-on of people agreeing whole-heartedly that the Oxford comma was something dear and important to them. It seemed to be an emblem of sorts. Somehow, someone got the idea that if you neglect to use the Oxford comma you must be dumb and crass, but if you are smart and elegant you will always include that extra bit of punctuation. And man, is that silly.

My own attitude toward the serial comma is the one I learned from the newspapers I've worked for: I usually leave it out.

Newspapers have to pay for every dot of ink and inch of paper they use, and when you consider all the commas that appear in a paragraph, article, or entire edition, the tiny amount of space that is saved by omitting any unnecessary one adds up. Newspaper editors leave out the serial comma unless to do so would cause confusion—and that caveat is important. If you don't use a serial comma in the following sentence, for example, your intended meaning would get confused: "I would like to dedicate this book to my parents, Mr. T. and Count Chocula." In this sentence you'd need to put that serial comma back in to make it clear that you're talking about three different referents: your parents, Mr. T., and Count Chocula. Unless your parents are Mr. T. and Count Chocula, in which case, you know, no judgment. We're all friends here. In any case, if the meaning won't be affected, you can leave the last comma out. Unless you want to leave it in. It doesn't matter. It's simply a matter of style. You can do what you like.

It bugs me that the self-appointed keepers of nerd culture have adopted this stupid cause. I have a feeling that they just enjoy knowing things like this; they like the sound of themselves telling someone what an Oxford comma is, and the image of themselves as a person with such refined taste that they have a preference in the matter. The existence of this preference is held up as proof of how quirky and smart and nerdy they are.

I guess Tumblr is a haven for nonsense like this, because I recently saw a meme roll past my dashboard that belongs in the same category as the bogus Oxford comma debate. It was a pretty photo of a row of books on a single white shelf hanging from a pretty blue wall—a fetish picture, if you will. Two or three of the books on the end had tipped over and were falling off the shelf, and the photo captured them mid-tumble. The meme maker had added a caption on top of the photo, like tourist postcards used to have. ("Greetings from Asbury Park!") This caption said, "Every time you watch an episode of *Jersey Shore,* a book commits suicide."

I found this powerfully irritating. What does it even mean? In what way could enjoying some pop culture bullshit possibly be harmful to your consumption of "higher" art, let alone cause the art itself to want to take its own life? I'm not ashamed to tell you that, as a person who loves reality TV and who grew up going "down the shore" in New Jersey every summer, I watched *Jersey Shore* with relish (though they never should have made that weird season in Italy. What was that?). I also read more books than the average American, according to recent surveys by Pew and Gallup (which found that, on average, Americans read between 14-17 books a year). Neither activity has interfered with the other, and in fact the two experiences probably enhance each other in ways that are surprising and useful. Like ... right now, actually. I have an opinion about this kind of snobbishness, and it's informed by my interest in language and writing just as much as it is by the 400 million hours my little sister and I logged in front of the TV as kids, watching junk and laughing like goofballs.

It's just so stupid. "A book." Which book? *Fifty Shades of Grey?* How about *The Turn of the Screw?* After all, Henry James' work belonged to the popular culture of his time. What I'm saying is, who decides what intelligence is, and what it looks like?

I think we all know who.

•   •   •

Some years ago now, when I was in my early twenties, I volunteered as an adult literacy tutor. I would take the train downtown and never even have to go outside to do this job, because the tutoring center was located in a commercial space in the big urban shopping mall that also housed the train station. I still remember the man who ran the center—Mike, a floppy-haired, melancholic social worker who didn't have time to properly train me in teaching adults to read, but let me observe him as he worked with a student and passed along some articles and books on the subject. I only lasted as a volunteer for a short time, under a year, because I found it so depressing, and for reasons I couldn't have predicted.

Illiteracy (like literacy) is a complicated concept and it is poorly understood. Some of us have an image of what it might look like that we got from corny sitcoms that tried valiantly to address social issues. On those shows, adults who can't read are depicted as closeted folks with a shameful secret. Their secret gets revealed one day when they have to read aloud a shopping list or a card from a relative, and everyone watches them struggle to figure out how the symbols on the page correspond to speech sounds. "Sounding out" is how children are taught to read, but this is rarely what happens when adults "can't read," though dyslexia and other learning disabilities can certainly cause such a problem that extends into adulthood. Even still, by the time most people are adults they have enough experience with making associations between words and their corresponding ideas, just to get by in everyday situations, that they usually have some idea of how words in their native language are rendered on the page. Functional illiteracy, as I learned, tends to take a much different form than not knowing how the sounds and signs match up. For example, the two people I worked with most closely when I was a tutor had something surprising in common. Both of them knew how to read but thought that they didn't.

There was Maritza, a Puerto Rican woman in her early thirties, probably—younger than I am now, I bet—with a skinny, lovely, sullen 13-year-old daughter whose name I can't remember now. Like adult learners of most subjects, Luz had a practical purpose for being there. She wanted to "learn to read" so that she could help her daughter do her homework. We used the homework assignments themselves as teaching tools, and as the three of us worked together—the daughter, who I don't remember ever saying a single word to me, came along to these sessions—I saw that Luz did have some difficulty with comprehension and benefitted from the conversations we had about the material after we read it together. But the much bigger issue was the impenetrability of the girl's completely stupid homework assignments, which out of the context of the classes they were based on, were almost impossible for me to understand. I can still remember one worksheet that was about weather systems, of all things. The questions were posed in the same dense and convoluted way that I remember badly worded assignments and instruction sheets from my miserable school days. It pissed me off so much that this kid, who needed help with basic reading skills, was not getting the attention she needed in school and instead was having her time wasted with this nonsense. Weather systems my ass.

As I got to know Maritza, I found out that she also had a son, just two years older than her daughter, but she was no longer parenting him in the same way; he'd had trouble with school too, she said, but she talked about that in the past tense and I didn't pursue the subject further. They lived in a rough area in North Philly and often got subway tokens from Mike in order to afford the trip to the center. They didn't have a phone so they took calls at her mom's a few blocks away. Maritza and her family were doing okay, but they were working with very limited resources and trouble was always at the door. It hurt me to see the complete confidence she put in the school, and the timid reverence with which she regarded the papers and books. Using the same bullshitting skills I employed when I was a student, I tried to help her do the assignments in the way that I thought the teacher wanted the questions answered, and kept my rage-opinions about the value of their content to myself.

The other person I worked with at the center was Major. Major was a smart, sad-looking Black guy in his late forties who had a job that was way below his ability level, washing dishes at a nice restaurant. He told me that he'd dropped out of high school in the ninth grade to stay at home with his mother, who was an alcoholic, because he was worried she wasn't safe by herself. When we met at the center, we read the newspaper together, taking turns reading articles out loud and then discussing them. He had no difficulty with the language itself, and his ability to talk about the ideas was superior to mine. We were both embarrassed by this, and I was totally confused. Why did this man think he didn't know how to read? After several sessions together, I told Major that I didn't think I had much to offer him and suggested he work toward taking the GED. The literacy center was set up to help people prepare for the test, but that too turned out to be a minefield; turns out, the GED is hard. A lot harder than sliding through school without learning much of anything, as any number of the people you know can probably tell you. The GED problem was just one of many reasons that the folks I met were feeling stuck in place.

I don't mind telling you that I was fucking astounded by what this experience taught me about our perceptions of ourselves in the world. I thought about all the over-validated dopes I've worked with (and for) in comfy, well-paying office jobs over the years. Almost all of them were white, and I'm sure many, if not most of them had a growing-up experience that was similar to mine: middle-class and safe. Forget worrying about "falling through the cracks," or busting your ass just to scrape by—they had every expectation that they would do well in life and very little reason to feel proud of this on a personal level, though most of them seemed to. I remember my little classmates in Catholic grade school, squirming with boredom in their scratchy uniforms, tucked into their old-fashioned desks. Almost all of those kids were white and middle-class like me. A few of them came from families that were too big or too broke to be comfortable—not enough attention at home, school clothes that went unwashed for too long—but to my knowledge none of us was truly poor. I remember listening to many of those kids struggle mightily to read passages aloud from their textbooks, but there's not a chance that any of those people reached adulthood believing that they didn't know how to read. Who knows, maybe some of them, now that we're all grown up, are acting like snobs on the internet, bragging about all the books they own and all the TV shows they've never seen.

It seems to me that the real reading lesson is written in invisible ink, and only the people with access to certain privileges, or the ability to mimic them, can see it. When it comes down to it, I don't care whether other people read or not, and I don't think that enjoying reading makes me better than people who don't. What I do care about, what I dearly wish, is that everyone had equal access to these things, but everyone doesn't. Not by a long shot. Of all of Nerd Culture's many sins, this one is probably the worst: As usual, the fancy people don't care about anyone but themselves.

All this complaining I'm doing is reminding me of a conversation I once had with a guy I worked with at a university, where I had a job as a research assistant. The position didn't require me to do any writing, but some of the people there, including this one supervisor of mine, knew that I work as a writer sometimes. He came and found me in the computer lab one afternoon and interrupted the stupid task I was doing to ask me about the Oxford comma. He'd heard a big deal being made about it on the Internet, he said, and now he wasn't confident that he was using it right.

To this day, this was one of the only real-life, in-person conversations I've ever had about the Oxford comma and the supposed controversy surrounding it, so I got kind of excited as I made my case. Instead of engaging me in the conversation he'd started, my manager startled me by saying, "Shhhh, relax." I think he chuckled a little too. His condescension made me so angry that cold fusion took place in my brain, which is dangerous, because I could have blown up the whole building. No way has that guy ever said the word *relax* to another man, at least not without expecting a fight.

But that's a whole 'nother conversation.

17.

Obsolete

A good few years ago now, when I was about to turn 30, I made a poetry book, a nifty little book with a kind of gimmick. (If you're going to try to get people to read your poems, a gimmick does not hurt.) Each poem was titled, and was ostensibly "about," a word of English that is no longer in use. A dead word. There were 26 of them, one for each letter of the alphabet, and I called the collection *Obsolete*.

I found the words by reading through the unabridged *Oxford English Dictionary*, in which every word of English, both past and present, is collected. My small local library has the full OED in its collection but it's a condensed version that fills three huge, tall books, instead of the 20 volumes the dictionary usually takes up. The pages from the longer version appear intact in the condensed one, only they've been photo-reduced to a tiny size so that four can fit onto each page. When I was working on my book, I sat at the library day after day, moving up and down the pages with the magnifying glass I borrowed from the library's front desk. I was hunting for obsolete words, waiting for the italicized obs. to appear under my magnifier, and when it did I read the definition to see if the idea of the word caught my fancy. When I found one I liked I wrote it down, and later I'd bring home my notebook of obsolete words and start working on a poem. A new poem about an old word.

When I was finished with all the research and writing for my book, I asked a friend of mine with a mostly-unused degree in graphic design to lay it out, and he produced this incredibly lovely design that was a kind of meditation on typography, on the letterforms themselves. He blew up each letter of the alphabet and used them as the background of the pages; the poems he nestled within and around the apertures and curves of the letters. The S's and U's and G's were like great architectural structures rising up from a city street. The design was beautiful and elegant and it shined my poems right up, making them appear cleaner and more perfect than they really were. I loved that the collection was not just a book of poems, but a book that was explicitly about language, all the way down to the letters themselves.

When I think about the book now, I feel fondly toward it, and find I'm able to remember the process of making it as being much more relaxed and considered than it actually was. The truth is, a kind of hysteria went into the creation of the little thing. The poems didn't come to me easily but were essentially wrenched out of my poor, dying laptop, and if it hadn't been for the costumey studiousness of my approach—my meditative walks to the library, my daily writing schedule, the damn magnifying glass—I don't think they would have gotten written at all.

Maybe that's more or less how all books get written, I don't know. It's a lot of work, so you do have to make yourself a schedule and stick to it. But when I look back on this time, I can remember the mental state I was in. There was something dogging me, something beyond my desire to see my work in print. I was trying to outrun a fear of failure, hustling to keep from wasting away in front of the TV or the internet. I felt like a loser, and I had felt that way for a while. And it was starting to break me down.

●　　　●　　　●

Depression is hard to understand and describe, and even though it's more acceptable to discuss it these days than it used to be, many of us don't really believe in it as an illness. Sometimes even I don't. There's so much guilt and self-blame coiled around the idea, it can feel like something you brought on yourself and should be able to shrug off—even though, at the same time that you're thinking these self-blaming, boot-strappin' thoughts, you're sitting in your dim, dirty bedroom for the third day in a row and your t-shirt has started to smell.

I can tell you what I felt like back then. Not precisely sad, or tired, or sick—though I did feel all three of those at once, to some extent—but dead. It was as if I had died, but for some reason my life hadn't actually, technically, stopped; a clerical error had been made, perhaps, some Grim Reaper's assistant with a sloppy ledger system had neglected to erase my name from one list and add it to the other. I had the eeriest sensation that I had fallen off the back of the jostling covered wagon of my own life and it had gone on trundling down its dirt path without me, leaving me behind.

Left behind, that's exactly what it felt like. There's this beautiful movie called *Broken English* and in it the Parker Posey character lives by herself and we can see, just from the meticulous way she dresses herself in the mirror, that her life is too quiet. She finally, grudgingly accepts an invitation to a party one evening and once she's there she thanks the host, saying "I was beginning to feel like the last person on Earth." That's what had happened to me, though I'm not exactly sure how. The wind whistled through the friendlessness of my existence. If I held still enough, remained quiet enough, all by myself in my silent apartment, I might have disappeared.

When I got the idea to write *Obsolete*, I was turned on by the idea of dead words for a few reasons. Not long before this, I had discovered traditional poetic forms, like cinquains and sonnets, and that some contemporary writers still used them. Though most of the poems in my book ended up being free-verse, the idea that those old forms could still have value was important to me. Lots of other almost-obsolete stuff appeals to me too, like glitchy TV screens with pixelated colors scrawled across them, or typewriters, which are beautiful objects but are now so entirely unnecessary that we only use them for fun (if your idea of fun is arduously pounding on a piece of metal). There's something really touching about a tool or a process that was invented solely for its usefulness—as opposed to something without a clear "use," like a piece of art—that is now, you know, pretty useless. Not old enough to be a proper antique, just old enough that you feel a little sorry for it, sitting there acting like it's still a real thing. Those wooden rolodexes and clunky VCRs, they're pitiful and noble at once, like the image of the old British gentleman who still expected to be addressed as Colonel, fifty years after the war.

It's trite but true, I think, now that I look back on it, to say that I was feeling pretty obsolete myself right about then. I had ramped up work on *Obsolete* soon after the regular newspaper column I'd been writing for several years was cut, my services no longer needed. I was shocked to find that after getting laid off, I felt a strange combination of heartbroken—as though a love relationship had ended or a person I cared about had died—and extraneous, like I could no longer justify my existence. For a long time, without quite realizing it, I had gotten most of my sense of self-worth from my idea of myself as a writer, and when it seemed like the world didn't want me to be a writer anymore I didn't know what my life was supposed to be.

Also, I felt old. All throughout my twenties I'd looked more or less the same, but that nice plateau gave way all at once and like a big old mudslide, I caught up with my real age. All of a sudden I was 30 and I looked it, if not older. Friends noticed, I could tell, people who I hadn't realized liked me, at least in part, because they thought I looked cute and bright and was fun to be around. All of a sudden they were liking me a little less now that my skin was splotchy and pale and my eyes were starey and my posture was slumped, and I had taken to wearing my "inside" clothes out in public. It seemed—and this is pretty damn true, I think— that every small area of my life affected every other one, so that once a major pillar had crumbled, the entire structure became wobbly and unsafe.

Seriously, I felt like shit. But the weirdest thing about all this is that it sounds silly to me now, even as I recall how painful it was. I was suicidal because I'd lost a job? I felt worthless because I was, and looked, older than 25? Yes, and yes. And no. I've managed depressive thoughts and excruciating anxiety since childhood, so I guess it's something chemical—and genetic, since I remember my dad darkening the house with his periods of "melancholy" very well, too. I think living through these difficult periods is just part of the human condition, and I also think that a certain sensitivity to pain like this is probably built into the artist's job description; I mean it's not exactly easy to plunge your emotional depths on a regular basis, to spend long periods of time in places that are very tempting to avoid.

In any event, for a while there, I felt lost. Without my paying writing job, I needed *Obsolete* to feel legitimate. I let it take up lots of time and pinned a great deal of hope on it—my smart book of poems about language, my cool book about words that were dead. Like me.

But let me tell you more about how the book came into the world. After my friend and I had laid it out, I hired another friend, who had recently apprenticed as a printer, to produce the book on an offset press. We chose a dark navy ink for the text, cream-colored paper for the inside pages, and a golden-yellow cover, all of which gave the book a richer look than plain old black and white, but for not much more money. A few months later the books arrived in the mail in a heavy cardboard box, which sat in my hall closet for the two years or so that it took me to sell them all. I'd pull out a handful at a time and bring them to zine fairs and craft shows, where the attractive design and nifty premise always drew some attention.

I set up shop at events like these often, and that book, the only "real" one alongside my photocopied zines, soon became my centerpiece. I was so proud of how it looked. For two whole years I heard myself give the same spiel: "It's an alphabet of poems inspired by obsolete words of English." I watched different kinds of people troop past my table, many of them passing it up for the knitted scarves or beaded jewelry that the other vendors had for sale. But a much smaller group of people, the ones who were maybe a little more like me, stopped for a moment, picked the book up shyly, and dug around in their pockets for a five-dollar bill. Some of those people wrote me emails and letters later, telling me they'd liked the poems or the idea behind them, or both. I also heard from people who had not bought the book from me, but had happened upon it at a friend's house or in a library in some indie arts space, or had received it as a gift. One girl wrote asking me to sell her a copy to send to her friend in Nairobi. She had her own copy, which she'd swiped from a friend at a tree planting camp in British Columbia. Her friend, the camp's cook, had originally gotten it from his ex in Australia. On another occasion, I did a reading at an event where a woman played her guitar and sang. Afterward, I gave the musician a copy of my book, and she kindly wrote a few months later to tell me that she'd been keeping the book on the windowsill in her bathroom, and that every visitor to her house had something nice to say about it. What a funny thing it was for me to imagine, all these books I'd made, out having their own experience of life—in wet Canada and sunny Kenya, in bathrooms and kitchens, resting patiently on some windowsill, ready to be opened again.

About a year and a half after I made the book I took some copies of it to a zine fair on a college campus in New Jersey. I wore my favorite zine fair dress, a red one that had a sort of sculptural shape to it, like a tank top attached to a balloon skirt. We set up our tables around the perimeter of a gymnasium and waited for the browsers to start filing in. After a while this cute, funny guy came over from his own table and danced around nervously in front of me, saying he was interested in my poetry book and asking if I did trades. I totally did trades, I said, so he gave me his "box set," which was the entire series of his charming, hand-drawn zine, housed in a box he'd constructed out of popsicle sticks, craft paint, and pipe cleaners. I treasured the quirky box and kept it on display in my living room, on the cabinet where I keep all my zine-making supplies. Some months later he wrote me an email inviting me to make an issue of his zine with him. In my issue I wrote about how I've always wanted to hug a big, fluffy bird, like a goose or a swan, and he drew a picture of me doing so.

We stayed in touch sort of spottily until he spent a week in Philly to look after his sister's cats, and our long-distance friendship bloomed into an up-close romance. Once we'd been together for a little while, Joe told me that after we'd met he'd kept my book beside his bed and read one poem a night, trying hard to imagine the inner life of the person who'd written them. He felt like he was falling in love with me through those poems, he said, and he had to try to find me and see if it would work for real.

We're getting married next month.

So that's the story with *Obsolete*. But there's something else I want to tell you about the words that inspired the poems. As I worked on the book, I got into the habit of googling the words I'd written about, just to see what, if anything, would turn up. To my surprise I found a number of them, floating out there on the sea of the internet, the weirder ones especially. Stiricide, for example, which means to be killed by a falling icicle, had been adopted as a username on blogs and social media sites—Reddit, OK Cupid, Twitter. I'll be damned, I thought. The words came back! Now that there is this need for people to name their online selves, there's a newfound use for interesting, unusual words. They might serve a different purpose than they did before, but the fact is, some of them are being used again.

See, I'd made a mistake, taking that word "dead" at face value. Language is so mutable, so fluid, so surprising, that I forgot it isn't actually alive. A non-living thing can't really die, which means words can only be dead statistically. A word that has been out of use for 200 years or so has been left behind, you might say, but to anyone who's been paying close attention—the editors at the OED, for example, or me, or you—it's still a word. It still counts.

And it can be brought back at any time.

Section
Two

Journalism

18

No Rooftop Was Safe:
The History of Philadelphia Graffiti

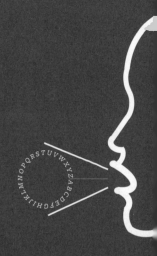

"All the kings are in the house!" Don Ameche Stallings says, beaming at his friends, men who were once some of the most notorious graffiti writers in the country.

For a time Stallings was a kind of mayor of graffiti, organizing the crews and their ragtag writers into a full-fledged movement. Some 25 years ago he proclaimed to the world by way of a can of spray paint: Master Prink 123 It's Me!

The kings have converged on the 2700 block of North Fifth Street, a corner that's seen its share of hustles and gang huddles and kids trying to get an easy beat, for a kind of family reunion.

Local filmmaker Brian MacDonald has lured Stallings to Taller Puertoriqqueno, the North Philly cultural center, on this bright, crisp Saturday morning to help showcase a graffiti encyclopedia project, Stallings, now 39, is working on. Today the "five elements of hip-hop" will be showcased (that's MCing, DJing, break-dancing, the human beat-box, and graffiti) as part of the hip-hop documentary MacDonald and Kim Waters are putting together.

Inside Taller Puertoriqqueno, a crowd is gathering for the show. Two skinny, fragile-looking white boys in full b-boy regalia are milling around, admiring Stallings' work under their breath. "That's bad, that's bad," one murmurs approvingly.

"That's the kid that emails me every day," Stallings says, amazed at what graffiti hath wrought.

The day wears on; the crew is working hard; and many MCs and DJs are getting their turn at bat. It's loud in here and the hall is bursting with the crazy energy that comes from trying to get noticed.

Toward the front of the room is Cornbread, a man who long ago learned how to get noticed without making a peep. Cornbread sits in front of two booming speakers, stretches out his long legs, and falls asleep.

•   •   •

"Graffiti started out as a love story," Stallings says, just as quotable as can be, and it's true.

"I was released from reform school in 1967," Cornbread, now 48, recalls. After spending ages 10 and 11 in what he calls, alternately, "school" and "jail," he was returned to the public school system. "While I was introduced I was scanning the class looking for the prettiest girl. I spotted her but I didn't know how to talk to her because all I knew how to talk was gangbanger-jitterbug talk."

So he set in motion what was surely one of the more determined wooing projects of the latter 20th century. He stole a look at her roster and arrived to all her classes before she did, writing "Cornbread loves Cynthia" on her desk. He also wrote it all down the block where she lived, and all along the bus route she took to school.

He befriended her as Darryl, which is why for a while she was dumbfounded as to who this Cornbread might be. He walked her home from school but had to stop a block short. Cornbread was something of a jitterbug himself, and Cynthia's father didn't want him around. One day she saw on one of his schoolbooks the same declaration she'd seen on her desk, and it was then she knew that Cornbread was one Darryl McCray.

"That's when she fell in love with me," he says.

Cynthia's father moved her to another school and away from him. But writing the many declarations of love had landed Cornbread a new obsession.

"I would go to the bus barns all night long writing on every bus in that depot," he says. "Riders would sit on the name Cornbread, go to work and see Cornbread, come home from work and see Cornbread again," he says. "I became obsessed with this name."

He'd picked up the name, incidentally, while he was locked up. His grandmother could make cornbread so delicious it tasted like cake, and he missed it. "How come y'all never fix no cornbread?" he would ask the cooks. The name stuck.

In 1971 a kid named Cornelius whom Darryl had known for a long time—he was no older than 17 or 18—was shot dead on the street. They used to call Cornelius Corn for short. The papers got the names mixed up and the story wrong, and next day on the bus Darryl read about his own death.

"I called the newspapers and said 'I'm Cornbread, and I'm not dead. You better straighten this out or I'm gonna tear this city up.' I knew it was up to me to bring my name back to life."

So he went to the Philadelphia Zoo and he cased the joint, watched where the zookeeper fed peanuts to the elephant and where he washed him down. The elephant was so domesticated he wasn't likely to cause a fuss. Early one Sunday morning Cornbread scaled the fence and sprayed "Cornbread Lives" on both sides of the creature.

And that's nothing. You should hear about the time he went to the airport to watch the Jackson 5 arrive for a concert. While the crowd's attention was riveted on the group, Cornbread tagged his name on a TWA 747.

Before long he'd started a trend, and Bread's friends—Dr. Cool and Tity Peace and the others—had become a crew.

•   •   •

The earliest Philly wall writing is called gangster-style, and for good reason. Graffiti, as we know it, sprang from the North Philadelphia street gangs of the 1960s, back when every few blocks constituted a different territory. Gang members would mark their ownership right on the walls, and to get someplace you had to be prepared to answer for yourself and where you came from.

Sub, a writer who grew up at 20th and Oxford and now owns a barber shop at 14th and Dover, remembers it well. "There was no good answer," he says. "They used to say that 'nowhere' was the biggest gang in the world."

Sub is tall and well-built with a round face and a devilish expression, like a sweet-looking 12-year-old who's a hairsbreadth away from flipping somebody the bird. He's just made a bleak statement about violence and fear, but his eyes are bright with the memory of getting one over on those guys. "Cornbread said the whole city was his turf. He united all the gang members."

Picture it: A baby-faced tough kid, well acquainted with the rules about turf and ownership, could roll down any block he chose.

Cornbread always had a little pack of followers with him, made up sometimes of 10 different guys from 10 different gangs. But while the members of rival gangs wrote with Bread during the day, at night they were still warring.

"It was the era of the street hustler, the pimp, the thief, and the tough guy," recalls Stallings. "I started seeing graffiti when I was 10, in 1972, on 10th and Thompson, which was a big gang corner. I'd see Little Sonny, Devil, and Otto when I walked past it every day to go to Harrison Elementary at 11th and Thompson." He and his fellow fifth graders would stare at old gangster hands scratched into his desk at school and pretend they were the bad guys. Within two years he'd obliterated his junior high school with the name Doctor Proctor.

Stallings didn't make this choice easily. His family was church-brought; he'd been a deacon. He eventually dropped out of school, he says, and started writing instead of praying. It wasn't always clear what it meant to be a man.

"My father kept a gun. He told me, 'If I'm not home, you're the man of this house. If anybody break in here, don't ask questions. Just unload.'" He was 13 then, and his father was just 32 when he died a year later. An alcoholic whose health was poor, he cut himself shaving one morning and the bleeding didn't stop. He was rushed to the hospital and never came home.

"I was mad at the world," Stallings says. "[Graffiti] was my way of getting even. This was my payback to the world."

He started bombing every chance he got with his partner Teaz. He whipped those writers into shape, getting the heads of all the best crews to operate under one name, the Children of Doom. He became a master of mimicry and could reproduce any hand he'd seen. He taught a lot of guys how to write.

"I was living with my mom at 10th and Master," Stallings says. "She didn't really know I was writing on walls. She called it the devil's handwriting." Today, Stallings is an evangelist minister for the Greater Canaan Church of God in Christ.

By the '70s, graffiti in Philadelphia was out of control. The city appointed a 20-man graffiti squad. A 1972 Camden Courier-Post article reported that it cost $1,000 a day to remove graffiti from the City Hall complex.

In 1971 a woman wrote to the Evening Bulletin "in white heat and in rage" over the problem. "Will the Liberty Bell be next?" she implored. Not quite—they had to wait until 1976 for that, when KAP the Bicentennial Kid slammed the Bell with his tag two weeks before the Fourth of July.

Philadelphia was the undisputed graffiti capital of the world, but to most people this was no badge of honor. The tags that covered the city were stylistically complex, nearly impossible to read, and communicated little more than urban decay to the average commuter. While some championed it as "folk art" or a kind of thwarted creativity, the vast majority of people, when they looked at graffiti, felt angry and discouraged.

"The city was tore up so bad that shit even got on my nerves," Sub says.

Even Cornbread, who'd left the city in 1974 for seven years to follow an acting career that never took off, couldn't believe his eyes when he came home again.

"When I got back the whole town looked like a war zone. It was a nuisance; it was a sight. I felt bad because I felt responsible," he says.

Wilson Goode's election pledge in 1983 was to clean the mess up, and in 1984 he initiated the Anti-Graffiti Network.

"Mayor Goode sent a letter to my house!" Sub recalls with glee.

The letter said Sub had ten days from the time he received it to turn himself in. "I bombed those ten days," he says, even getting off an especially good one: "Ha ha hee hee you can't catch me." When he did report himself, it was for the promise of a job.

"When the city addressed the issue of graffiti it was already dead," Stallings says. "There was no place to write your name because the city was already so marred."

Around that time graffiti moved to New York and got itself a fancy new association. No longer a gang thing, wall writing was now a hip-hop thing. Graffiti became hopelessly intertwined with the new urban party culture when Afrika Bambaataa's Zulu Nation took a troupe of DJs, breakers, MCs and graff writers on the road. In 1983 Henry Chalfant's groundbreaking film *Style Wars* solidified the association in the public's mind. Hip-hop sensibilities spent the next 15 years mushrooming out to middle America, and while graffiti hasn't gone away, it's never been the same since.

"The scene sucks now," laments Soul, a young graffiti writer and DJ at Drexel's radio station, WKDU. But while he decries the art-school kids from the suburbs who have infiltrated the culture, he would never deny the legitimate white graffiti experience: "Them cats was straight thugs."

• • •

In a suit and a silver BMW, Suroc doesn't look like he was ever once one of those scruffy white street kids. Today he's a family man, a salesman, and a musician. But back when he sat in his fifth grade classroom, thumbing through a math book filled with doodles and tags a decade old, he was already deeply knowledgeable of the currency in being tough. Graffiti was like a varsity letter, something worth earning.

"Nobody really aspired to be a good boy in my neighborhood," he says, referring to the Overbrook section of the city where he grew up. "Whatever art education you can say I had was probably trying to copy Spiderman and draw on my own the comics I would get from the local drugstore," Suroc (who has asked that his real name not be used) says, adding that he always had an affinity for the bad guys.

By 1983 Suroc's finely tuned—and oft-practiced—ideas earned him the title "style king." In Stephen Powers' book *The Art of Getting Over*, Powers recalls calling him "Hollywood" "because he was so good at being conceited." Suroc was a tough kid, but he was also a smart kid, with big dark eyes that didn't miss a beat and a black notebook full of high-concept ideas about graff and the things it could say to people.

His battered book shows the synthesis of many masterpieces, yet an admonishment blazes off one page as if in anticipation of a snooping journalist some 15 years ahead of time: "It's graffiti; don't call it art!"

"The best graffiti involves a sense of perspective, and you only get a sense of perspective by involving certain emotions in the work—such as humor, drama, tragedy," Suroc says now. "And thievery. I think being able to steal ideas, to take text and manipulate text into your own ego and your own reinvention of imagery is important, and I don't see that as an artistic statement. I see it as a graffiti statement."

Some of the stuff he stole was more concrete than ideas. "I spent a lot of time fencing and doing a lot of burglary when I was a kid because that was kind of tradition too," he says. "There's more marriage between the culture of hustling and graffiti than there is of hip-hop and graffiti. Before the assault of hip-hip on America, there were punk kids and skate kids who were down with getting up with graff and getting up with the hustle."

Back then a bottle of Night Train, a few joints, some good music— the Slits, Gang of Four, the Clash—and a few friends was all he needed to fuel a night's outing. With the club he started, Inner City Youth, he harnessed the best piecing, or painting, talent in the city for a time. "The great clubs of Philly were temporal," he says wistfully. "That's an inherent property of graffiti—that it's not to last."

Of course not. Those kids never expected the graffiti they wrote to stick around forever. It wasn't created with the kind of arrogance with which the life around them had been constructed: the brick monoliths, the slapdash housing projects, the leering billboards. There's a special kind of bravery in being that young and invincible, but at the same time having a Zen-like wisdom about death that kids who grow up a little too fast always have. Graffiti's currency is the name, but it traffics in more than a thoughtless assertion of ego. It doesn't merely shout: "LOOK AT ME!" but, simply, look.

No. Look again. Keep looking. None of this will last forever.

19

Ye is Ye Old The

If you were to walk in downtown Philadelphia, south on 19th Street and just past Ludlow, you'd notice a sign bearing the words "Ye Olde Clean'ry." And if you haven't seen this place you've no doubt seen ones like it before. Signs like this make you imagine your shirt is being hand-scrubbed in tin tubs of fire-heated water, when really they'll join all the other shirts from all the other cleaners for the off-site assembly-line treatment at Kim's a few blocks away.

So what are we to make of this word ye?

I'll tell you. In today's English the sounds at the beginning of the words "the" and "thick" are both represented with the spelling "th." But they sound different—one has a "voice" in it and the other is silent—and many years ago, Middle English had two separate letters for them, called thorn and eth. Thorn and eth originally found their way into English as runes, the Germanic alphabet used in the British Isles from the Fourth to Seventeeth centuries. (To give you some context, Germanic people conquered most of Celtic Britain during the years 400-800, which resulted in the creation of the English language. The runic alphabet was used all over northern Europe, Scandinavia, and Iceland, but scholars don't agree on where it originated. A lot of conquering and sacking went on back then. It's anybody's guess.)

Thorn and eth remained in the English alphabet for a long time. In the Middle Ages the Latin alphabet replaced the runes, but when scribes made the transliterations they simply kept on using thorn and eth because the Latin alphabet had no equivalents.

Then in around 1450, good old Gutenberg showed up with his printing press. He and all the other early printers were from the Continent, and they had no letter to represent the English "th" sounds because their languages didn't use those sounds; they're actually very rare. So they chose one to represent both, the thorn, and substituted it with the letter that looked most like it: y. Ye for the (as well as yt or yat for that) appeared in printed manuscripts up through the Eighteenth century. There was no confusion at the time: Context told readers which y was being used.

But more time passed, and using the letter y to represent the thorn fell out of favor. Nowadays, "ye" is used instead of "the" to impart a sense of history, and the shopkeepers who put it in their names imagine they've given the names an instant pedigree. So the next time you take your clothes to the upscale cleaners, or have a cup of chai at Ye Fancy Olde Tea Shoppe, you can accuse them of putting on airs—but not of misspelling.

20

The Words Go Round and Round and They Come Here

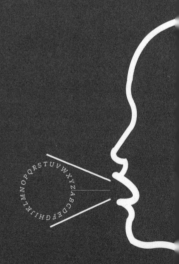

Have you ever seen voice-recognition software at work? Once you have it running on your computer you just start talking, and your words appear on the screen as though a phantom stenographer were typing them—or like a player piano that makes text instead of music.

Kurt Newman is a person who makes music—an improvisational guitarist, to be more precise—and one day he watched with fascination as one of his professors used a voice-recognition program to write a paper. He wondered: What would a program like that do with guitar music? Maybe it would treat it as a voice, and attempt to make sense of the sounds as words in English. He decided to find out, and the resulting experiment was just the kind of collaboration he and his wife, poet Michelle Detorie, had been trying to find.

Detorie, who lives with Newman in Goleta, Calif., is a 2007 National Endowment for the Arts literary fellow. Her big interest is in divination, the ancient practice of reading signs in nature to answer questions or predict the future.

"Divination is an attempt to learn or figure out something by interpreting omens or some sort of data: tea leaves, ashes, entrails, the movements of animals, weather, and other things," Detorie told me. Astrology is a kind of divination; so is feng shui. She was initially interested in divination practiced by women, and she wrote a series of poems on the subject. One form that particularly captured her imagination was daphnomancy, in which a diviner burns branches of a laurel tree and interprets the sounds made as they crackle on the fire.

For some time Detorie and Newman had wanted to bring their music and poetry together, but nothing they'd thought of seemed quite right. They didn't want the music to be a simple backdrop for the text, nor did they want to write poems that interpreted the music in an obvious way. Perhaps using this artificial-intelligence tool as a kind of divining rod was the answer.

So Newman found one of the less expensive programs on the market, ViaVoice, and bought it on eBay for about $20.

"Michelle and I figured that the cheaper the software, the more likely it was to produce weird, and thus artistically interesting, glitches," Newman said.

Then they primed it by feeding it language. "You read passages into the computer, you feed the software documents," Detorie said, explaining how ViaVoice works.

"For the dictation process I tried reading in funny voices. Kurt tried playing his guitar into the machine, but it didn't really work for whole passages. For documents, I fed it all sorts of stuff—glossaries from art and biology textbooks, poems, articles from Wikipedia. I wanted to sort of stuff it with interesting vocabulary and different types of grammatical structures."

When the software was ready to be put to use, Newman and Detorie sat in front of their computer and Newman began to play his guitar. As he made music, the machine spat out "incomprehensible chunks of text," Detorie said—real words of English that looked like word salad, rather than sentences with semantic meaning.

That's when she stepped into the role of diviner. As the text was being generated, she looked for patterns and meaning and altered, amended, and shaped it into lines of poetry. Detorie and Newman even treated some of their sessions like real acts of fortune-telling, asking questions of the universe and looking for answers in the text.

"Most were questions we found on the Internet, like, 'My daughter is always crying; what is the problem?' Mostly we just picked questions that we liked."

The resulting poems are most noteworthy for their odd language, which, perhaps unsurprisingly, has a strong musical quality. "Owl on a low howl in a catacombed cave," goes the lilting first line of the poem "An Alliance of Grammar. "

The daphnomancy project has been performed live in Austin, Texas, and Detorie has collected a number of the poems and arranged them into a chapbook, which she sells on her shop at Etsy.com.

That, incidentally, was how I discovered the project, landing on it by accident as I plinked around on the site one day, shopping for a Christmas present. You wouldn't call that divination, I guess, just good luck, and an ear tuned to whatever in the universe I might be able to overhear.

21.

A Life Less Ornery

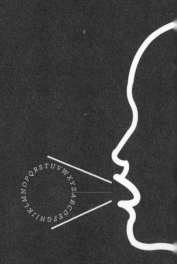

On October 16, 1758, Noah Webster was born in Hartford, Connecticut, the son of a farmer and weaver. He grew up to edit the first American dictionary, a project that took him 27 years to complete. His book was special because it wasn't just a speller for Americans to use—it was a record of the English used by Americans, which in colonial times was already distinct from British English.

During the time I spent in Ireland, I was delighted to hear all manner of Dublinisms being used. (The slang for being drunk alone could fill a book. Flootered, legless, bollixed, paralytic, stocious—they were all so clever and funny and absurd.) But apparently I, too, sounded funny to them. One day I was taking a walk with a friend when out of the blue he asked me, "Do you ever use the word ornery?" Hm. "Yeah, when it applies," I told him, thinking of the disagreeable shop girls in just about every store I'd been to in the city that day.

Turns out, ornery is an American word, which my friend knew but I didn't until I got back to my temporary home and looked it up in my housemate's (British) dictionary. It put ornery's date of birth at around 1816, and said the word comes from a variation of the pronunciation of the word ordinary, which then picked up a negative connotation. And indeed, we've all considered the word ordinary to be an insult at one time or another. Who wants to be just like everybody else?

Not Noah Webster. Instead of becoming a farmer he went to school, then to Yale, and later studied law. But he wasn't all that impressed with those American schools, which relied on books from England. He thought Americans should learn from their own books, so he wrote *A Grammatical Institute of the English Language*, a huge success that was outsold only by the Bible and, over the course of several years, taught millions of American kids how to read and write. A rebel word nerd; gotta love that.

At the age of 43 Webster began compiling his dictionary. Some peculiarly American spellings he included remain in use today, such as color instead of colour, catalog for catalogue, and plow for plough. Some of them didn't catch on, like wimmen for women (but try telling that to Mary Daly).

Webster had contempt for Samuel Johnson and his dictionary, partly because it included rude words like fart, and he set out to do a better job. To be sure, Webster's had 70,000 words to Johnson's 40,000, and it included a pronunciation guide, which Johnson hadn't attempted. Unfortunately Webster took a weird approach to word histories. He believed that all languages derived from an original one spoken by Adam and Eve, so he tried hard to show that English words had developed from the Biblical tongue through Hebrew, which is, um, wrong. When the Merriam brothers bought the rights to publish Webster's dictionary they hired a scholar to rewrite the etymologies.

And that's the story of how America came to have its very own dictionary. Why don't we all grab our *Merriam-Webster's,* learn a funny word, and surprise and amaze our friends and coworkers by putting it to use. Mine's pettifoggery, but you can use it too. The dictionary belongs to the people, people.

22

Talking the Talk

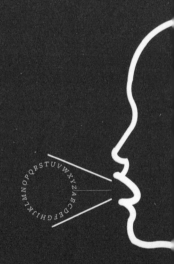

I'm standing in the Whisper Booth and it's airless and cramped, like an upright coffin. The thick foam on the walls is supposed to make it soundproof, but when the door closes the booth makes a sucking sound like it's sealing shut, like a freezer, and the pressure in there seems to tug on my eardrums. It doesn't feel that great.

I look through the booth's window and see Joanne Joella staring back at me, nodding, her dangling earrings bobbing with encouragement. She's like a doctor, telegraphing the phrase This won't hurt a bit. Joanne is a professional voice coach, and she has promised to help me sound more fancy. If I follow her guidelines and practice my exercises, she's assured me, I can learn to lose my Philly accent.

First, though, she needs to hear it. That's why I'm in the booth, with an enormous softball of a microphone in front of my mouth and a script in my hand. In the two years since she opened JoellaArts, Joanne has asked hundreds of clients to read this script. Most of her business comes from helping actors and TV personalities who want to lose their local twangs, something she's done as a vocal coach for more than 30 years. Lately, though, she has noticed more regular folks signing up for a visit to her Whisper Booth than ever before. In fact, I recently read in the *New York Times* that non-actors around the country are hiring voice teachers and speech pathologists for "voice styling." I was embarrassed to realize that I kind of agreed with the *Times* reporter, who wrote rhetorically: "Why shouldn't a richer, more sonorous voice be one more item on the checklist to perfection?" I've never been much for the idea of perfection, but a little personal improvement couldn't be a bad thing.

Growing up, I didn't realize there was a Philly accent. It was just the way we tawked. I don't have the most pungent regional accent, but it's there. And I'm well aware that, when in its full flower, the accent sounds something like the nasal Baltimore one you may know from John Waters movies. ("Dawn Davenport is eating a meatball sandwich right out in class. And she's been passing noootes!") My mom's relatives down in the old neighborhood call water wooder (okay, so do I) and they pronounce beautiful like it's two words (beauty-full). We all complain about people who have an "addytood," which is pretty much everyone here.

But I've always lived in and around Philly, never any further away than ten miles from where I grew up, and I sound more or less like everyone I know. I haven't really had much impetus to change.

Eventually, though, I began meeting people who let me know they thought I sounded funny. After graduating from high school I relocated all of five miles away for college. One day in a linguistics class, after I'd just finished pontificating on the language diversity in Papua New Guinea or something, this woman, a Ph.D. candidate from not-Philadelphia smiled smugly and announced to the room: "Oh, Katie. Your vowels are so cute."

For the first time in my life, I felt ashamed of how I sounded. She wasn't just commenting on the way I talked; she was commenting on who I was. She was calling me local, but not in a good way: more like small-town, provincial, un-self-aware.

Like every other insult that's ever been lobbed at me, this one hasn't entirely gone away. When I'm talking with people from out-of-town—and over the last several years, there have been more and more people from out-of-town moving here—I can feel myself trying to remember the "right" way to say things, and adjust my vowels accordingly. When I enrolled in Joella's seven-week "Freeing the Natural Voice" course, I did it for the same reason the *New York Times*-reading strivers do things—to try to build a better version of myself. With Joanne's help, I planned to find the Philly in my voice and pull it out by the roots.

•　　　•　　　•

Back in the Whisper Booth, I take a deep breath. I need to relax, Joella says, so that my "regional sounds" can flow. I start to read:

"At Pep Boys, people come in all the time just to get their batteries tested..."

I sound professional, anchorly. If there are regional sounds in there, I can't hear them.

"If the battery holds the charge well, the unit display will read 'good battery.' ..."

Easy. Smooth. I make batteries sound like dessert, like sex.

"If not, it will read 'bad battery.' ... "

I finish, push open the door, and look confidently at Joanne, this earthy woman with close-cropped hair who looks very hip, very San Francisco. She doesn't look like she's ever talked about going downashore.

"It's the moment of truth!" she announces, her own voice so crisp and sophisticated that she sounds like Greta Garbo. She hits the PLAY button on her computer and—oh jeez, my voice comes crackling out of the speakers like I'm yelling into a bullhorn: *"AT PEP BOIZE, PEOPLE COME IN AWLATIME JUSTA GET THUR BATTERIES TESTED. ... "*

"Oops!" Joanne says, turning down the volume. Oops indeed. The Katie in the speakers sounds much different from the Katie in my head. Joanne hits play again, quieter this time, and I can hear it, oh God: Ahunnertollers. I sound like my dad's cousin Jimmy. Nicest guy you'd ever wanna meet, but he's a tough, gravel-voiced, former beat cop who still rules the tumble-down neighborhood he grew up in. And he's like, 70. This is nowhere near the dulcet tones I was aiming for.

I bark out a laugh, trying to mask the same embarrassment I felt in class that day when, without my realizing it, my roots were showing.

"Do you hear that?" Joanne says, going to rewind the player on her screen.

"What?" I ask. This was beginning to feel like seeing a horrible photo of yourself and wishing you could hide in your room for the rest of the day.

"The nasal quality of that vowel," she says, and plays it over again. If not, it will read bee-ad battery. BEE-AD. Ugh.

"How did I not know I sounded like that?"

"Most people can't hear their own accents," Joanne says. She picks a folder up from her desk and takes out a diagram of the facial muscles and shows me how tension in the chin and jaw creates those nasal sounds. I can fix that, I think. Lighten up the tension, though that's probably easier said than done.

"Then there's the dark L," Joanne says, darkly. Despite my training in linguistics, I can't quite remember what that is. She reads my expression and imitates—exaggeratedly, I think, I hope—the way I say the word all. *Awwwl.* I'm "backplacing" the vowel sound, she explains, gargling it in the back of my throat.

"You need to restructure your tongue's muscle memory," she says. There are exercises I can do, and she promises that I'll begin to see progress if I do them for a few weeks. But it all sounds difficult and tiring, and a little creepy. I've never really thought of my tongue as a muscle, let alone one I could exercise. Furthermore, there is a lot more for me to try to "fix" than I'd anticipated.

"Also, honey," Joanne says gently. "I think you have a little bit of a lisp."

•   •   •

Joella's voice studio is located in a modest neighborhood about a 15-minute bus ride from where I live. The area is comfortable and down-to-earth, made up mostly of blocks of row-houses with little markets on their corners. The school itself is housed in a beautiful colonial building that was built a few years before the American Revolution. It's made of white plaster and has tiny black-shuttered windows, and when I approach it I can almost see the candle in the window, the full skirt of the woman of the house as she brushes past. The house is nicer than the ones that surround it, but that's what happens in these old neighborhoods. New things get added, but the old things don't always fall away.

During my first lesson, Joanne made me trill my tongue. The idea was to move my L-sounds from my throat all the way out to the tip of my tongue, where they belong. Trill for 30 seconds. Rest. Trill. Rest. I sounded like Catwoman, or so I thought.

This time around is the Lip Buzz. I am to buzz my lips—in essence, do raspberries—for several minutes a day. This, she says, will strengthen my embouchure, the shape of my upper lip, which is a word I know from playing the flute as a kid. A stronger embouchure will make my enunciation clearer. No more hunnertollers. Maybe, hopefully, no more lisp. (I've been trying not to think about the lisp.)

And now Joanne hands me the Denasality Exercise, a printout of the poem "Lay of the Deserted Influenzaed." The poem has been rewritten in the voice of a person with a severe cold: "Doe, doe! I shall dever see her bore!" Joanne says that talking like my nose is blocked will help me break my habit of sending air to my nasal passages, thus eliminating my Philly whine.

Over the next several weeks, as I buzz and trill—while filing my nails, while doing the dishes—I do start to hear a change. I've been using my old tape player to record myself reading the exercises—I don't have software to record myself like Joanne does—and when I play it back (always with the volume low, half-wincing) I begin to hear a subtle change. I definitely don't sound as much like my dad's cousin Jimmy, which is nice, I guess. Having this more neutral way of speaking does sound more sophisticated and less provincial. But there's something eerie about this transformation that I hadn't counted on. It isn't only that I don't sound like I'm from Philadelphia; it's that now, I sound like I'm not from anywhere at all.

The journalist Robert MacNeil, of the *MacNeil Lehrer Report*, wrote a wonderful book called *Do You Speak American?* To research it, MacNeil (who is Canadian) traveled around the country to take a closer look at the popular notion that people are losing their regional accents because of the homogenizing influence of mass media. Linguists had already dismissed this idea as hooey, and after talking to folks from Texas to Maine, MacNeil does, too. Why? He writes, "People treasure their local accents precisely because where they come from, or where they feel they belong, does still matter." It gets me thinking: If I no longer sound like where I'm from, will I remember where I belong?

The last time I meet with Joanne, we sit in the waiting area of her studio, where she has set a massive pub-style oak table. She's impressed with my progress: I've gotten rid of the bee-ad, my embouchure is stronger, and my wooder is wider.

"It's not that different from the way athletes work," Joanne says. "You can train your vocal cords, your tongue, all your speech ah-gans—" She stops abruptly, looking as mortified as though she's just passed gas.

Well I'll be damned. Underneath her Greta Garbo get-up, Joanne Joella has an accent, too. That's when we start to get a little more real. She tells me how she grew up in a working-class family, a townie in a snooty college town in southern Massachusetts, where she always felt like "a skunk at the garden party." But she had a singing voice, and she learned how to use it. She left home—and her accent—at eighteen and never looked back. She's proud of this, I can tell, but she looks sad about it too.

Now that I've finished with my lessons, there's only one step remaining in my makeover. I've got to try out my fancy new voice in public. With strangers. I invite my mom to join me for drinks at our favorite dive bar up the street.

When the server comes over I visualize pursing my lips as I pronounce my order. Wings with dipping sauce, please. I have to be especially careful with that word sauce. Soss. Not saws. Soss. I say it in my head before I say it out loud: "With dipping soss please." (See? *Fancy*.)

"Want me to bring you some wooder, too?" the waitress asks. It's Kathy, the same lady we've been talking to here for years. I remember when she got married, remember finding out that her husband was in my sister's class in grade school. For just a moment I don't say anything because it's as if my mind is stuttering, like it can't believe it spent that much time agonizing over how to pronounce some words I already knew how to say. I'm supposed to be feeling smart and worldly in my new voice, but I don't. I feel stupid, like I walked into this dump wearing a ball gown. My perfect pronunciation isn't impressing anyone here.

That's when I remember the story Joanne told me about one of her students, a hockey coach who wanted to erase his Philly accent so he could get work as a sports announcer. The only trouble was, when he lost his accent, he lost his credibility. No one at the local games believed he knew anything about hockey, not when he sounded like *Masterpiece Theater*. To be taken seriously in Philadelphia, he needed to sound like a Philadelphian.

And in that moment, I decided to save my new voice for elsewhere. For linguistics classes with snobs, or out-of-town job interviews. It's nice to think that I know how to switch when I need to, but much nicer to learn that I don't always want to.

"Wooder, hon?" the waitress asks again, her eyebrows raised this time. She's the nicest girl you'd ever wanna meet but her attytood is about to come out. But you know, I've always kind of liked that in a person.

"Yeeah," I say. "Wooder sounds great."

23

Dictionary in Reverse

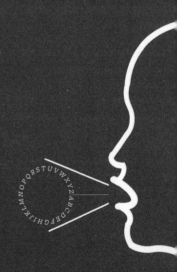

Do you know what a reverse dictionary is? Just what it sounds like, really—you look up the definition and get the word, rather than the other way around. They're meant to be used when you're groping for the perfect word for a concept or an object that you can describe, but can't name. Do a Google search: There are lots of reverse dictionaries online.

It seems to me that making a digitally-searchable dictionary would be much harder than making a paper-and-ink one, since digital searches are necessarily so much more open-ended. The creator would have to try to imagine a huge range of ways that people might use to describe each idea.

In playing around with some online reverse dictionaries I found that they usually work, in that they will provide the word you want, but in so doing they also spit back a long list of possibilities to choose from, some of them much more ridiculous than they are useful. I've listed some of the weirder results—not to make fun of the dictionaries' inadequacies, because I find them clever and worthwhile—but as an experiment in thinking about words and their meanings.

From the top 100 search results for "A person who falls in love easily":

drip
sucker
connoisseur
writer

From the top 40 search results for "A place to call home":

address
hell
here

No. 57 from the search results for "To look on the bright side":

speculum

No. 1 from the search results for "Tears of happiness":

overflow

24

The Way We Read Now

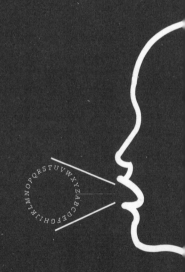

Two recent studies from the National Endowment for the Arts (*Reading at Risk* and *To Read or Not to Read*) found that Americans are reading less, and less well, than they used to. The studies have prompted much discussion: What does it mean for our culture and what can be done about it? Some of those who have joined the conversation are asking yet another question, one that might fairly be framed as a challenge: How do we define reading?

As media change, so do the ways in which we read, argues N. Katherine Hayles, literature professor at the University of California and editor of *Electronic Literature: New Horizons for the Literary* (University of Notre Dame, March 2008).

"We shouldn't confuse 'reading' with codex books," she said in a recent interview. "We need a broader definition of the function of reading and the sort of literacy necessary for reading."

A CD accompanying Hayles' book ("what we might think of as sample readings for major works in the field") drives home the point. Among other examples of new literature, it includes the first episode of "Inanimate Alice," a computer game-like narrative featuring a young, globally and digitally astute girl growing up in the 21st century.

"Inanimate Alice" has three creators: Kate Pullinger, a novelist, screen writer, radio script writer, and faculty member of the Creative Writing and New Media Department at De Montfort University in Leicester, England; Chris Joseph, a digital artist, writer, and composer who co-created the digital novel *The Breathing Wall* with Pullinger and Stefan Schemat, and Ian Harper, producer and CEO of BradField House, a new-media production company in London.

It's not surprising, given these many combined gifts, that "Alice" is lushly cinematic. As the first episode opens we hear eerie static, like a radio trying to connect. The audio clue is apt; in many of poor Alice's adventures she is scared and lost. At first Alice is eight years old, living in a remote part of China, where her father is "looking for oil." But he has been gone from their camp for days, and she and her mother take a harrowing trip on a bumpy rural road to look for him. Frenetic moving images and

Joseph's dark electronic music evoke a visceral reaction: This girl is in danger.

And it keeps happening. In the second episode, both parents are missing, leaving her alone in a cabin on a mountain in the Alps as night—and heavy snow—begins to fall. These narratives resolve themselves, but we're left with the twitchily uneasy feeling that something much larger is wrong.

Perhaps most interesting is that we never see Alice herself, only artistic representations of the things she sees and feels. To watch the story unfold we must interact with the pink handheld game player she takes with her everywhere. She uses it to talk to Brad, an animated character she made herself and considers her only friend.

These early audio and visual clues unfold over the course of ten episodes (only three are completed) to tell the larger story of a woman who becomes a successful computer game designer.

Some of the story's elements have grown out of digital culture (games, dynamic web design, computer-aided music composition). But the creators of "Alice" say their goal was to mimic and build on the experience of reading a book.

"For me, Alice is an attempt to carve out a space in our rather noisy media world for a kind of online reading," Pullinger said from her home in London. "It incorporates text, sound, and image, but in some ways it bears quite a close relation to reading a book. I'm really interested in creating a story where people will want to do the equivalent of turning the page."

Pullinger said the same elements that drive momentum in a book are present in the digital realm: narrative, character development, atmosphere, and space.

"Literature is about two things, really: our need for story, and great writing, beautiful writing," she said. "I guess when people worry about the face of literature, that is the element that they're talking about: somebody who really knows how to put those words on the page. But even that in itself has all kinds of different possible meanings."

Hayles compares "Inanimate Alice" to the illuminated manuscripts of William Blake. "He produced and conceptualized the books he wrote, and no one doubts that this had a profound influence on their meaning," she said.

"Alice" has found reception in different realms, including the classroom, and has been translated into Spanish, Italian, French, and German. It's a featured project in the European Year of Intercultural Dialogue 2008 and has been exhibited as a piece of digital art in several countries and screened at film festivals. It's all part of the multimodality, multimedia, multitasking reality for young readers, which "doesn't need to be viewed as a threat," said Pullinger.

"In many different ways we're at quite a critical point right now," she said. "The Internet is going to become increasingly a visual medium, with YouTube and people watching television online. This is the moment for creating a kind of new literature—which sounds grand, but in a modest way that's what 'Alice' is trying to do.

"We need to get on with that now."

25

Genderswap the Patriarchy

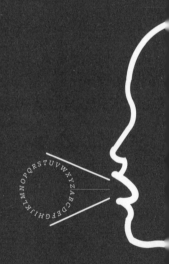

Do you ever wonder how much our ideas about gender really shape the way we see the world? Danielle Sucher did. So last November, she created Jailbreak the Patriarchy, a "genderswapping" extension she wrote for Google's web browser, Chrome. The app, when installed and turned on, automatically switches masculine and feminine pronouns and other gendered words on every website the user visits. Try it and you'll find yourself visiting a strange new world, one where most fashion bloggers are men but most of the successful designers are women, where the president is a woman too, and where the hero of the *Twilight* franchise is pregnant with his first demon baby.

A beautifully simple idea, Jailbreak helps suss out stubborn gender-based prejudices that afflict even the most enlightened among us. But there's a lot of humor here, too, as users soon found out.

Arts and culture site Flavorwire reported testing the extension on an article from the nefarious men's magazine AskMen.com, which yielded this gem: "You hear this over and over again: Nice girls finish last. Men don't want a nice girl; they want the jerk, the bad girl. So you think to yourself, "I've got to learn how to be a complete player. I've got to learn how to put men down."

Even the bugs are delightful: The extension launched the week the Penn State football case went public, and someone named Joe "Materno" was at the center of the controversy.

Sucher, a Brookyln-based attorney, says her program is a work in progress, with each micro-decision bringing up its own set of questions. Take, for instance, her decision not to change gender-specific insults.

"Should I swap bitch with stud? Something else?" she mused in an email interview. "What about slut or whore, which are generally seen as gendered (though don't necessarily have to be)? It's a tangled mess, and I ultimately just don't think it's necessary to swap those in order to wake people up."

One early user noticed that Sucher hadn't switched the words penis and vagina, either. In other words, the program swaps gender, not sex. This was a conscious choice as well.

"I really didn't want Jailbreak to be cis-centric," Sucher explained.

Another user requested a gender-neutral version that would change all gendered pronouns to "they" and "their." In response Sucher made her code available on github, a hosting site for collaborative software projects, so that anyone with the interest can tweak the extension to their liking.

Sucher, who has her hand in a diverse range of creative projects—she's also a jewelry artist, an urban beekeeper, and a food blogger—has no previous background in programming. (She joked that the last program she wrote was a tic-tac-toe game for her eighth grade Pascal class.) She considered Jailbreak a learning opportunity, she said.

What else has designing the extension taught her?

"I think I've mostly learned a bit more about some of my own blind spots. When a description of a gendered person jumps out at me as odd, checking whether I have the extension running occasionally leads me instead to the realization that I have some unconscious biases left to work out."

26

The La-La Theory

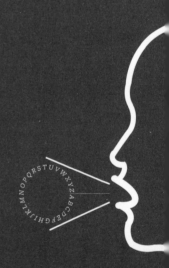

If you recall, for the year or so in Dublin I lived in a comically tiny rented room in Philip's house. Philip was a handsome, middle-aged English guy with floppy hair and Peter Pan Syndrome. He painted big, dour portraits of people in oils for a living.

Philip's house was really just two rooms with a tiny kitchen in the back, but he'd done work on it and created a second half-floor up near the ceiling, which he used as his own lofted bedroom—or just *bed*, really, since the space was too short to stand up in all the way. On the other side of the wall from Philip's bed was mine, also lofted and so close to the ceiling that lying there felt like being buried alive.

Philip loved classical music, and he had an expensive sound system installed in his bedroom. One morning I was awakened in my coffin-bed by the most ethereal music drifting over my head, sobbing strings in a minor key. For a long time I lay there, just listening.

"What was that music you were playing this morning?" I asked Philip later, when we bumped into each other (literally, practically) in the kitchen. "It was so beautiful. It was so *sad*."

"So would you be too, if you were from Estonia," he said in the peeved way he said most things, and went on to lecture me about twentieth-century European history and communism. Later, I read the CD's liner notes and learned that the music was made by the composer Arvo Pärt; I've since sought out more of his music and continue to be amazed by it.

The point of this story, though, is that the phrase *so would you be too* got lodged in my thoughts, where it played over and over, the way a song does, until it began to sound like a song. It had a certain rhythm to it, I guess. I began to wonder what made this happen. What makes something sound "like music"? Another way to ask this might be, What makes music, music?

A paper written by psychologist Diana Deutsch at U.C. San Diego looks at these very questions. Deutsch writes that one day she was listening to a recording of her own voice and, when she played one phrase in isolation over and over, it began to sound like she had sung it. The phrase was "sometimes behave so strangely," and you can find a video on Youtube of a classroom of kids singing along to it. It totally does; it sounds like singing, but only after you've heard it several times in a row. It's an effect that a million DJs have made use of already, incorporating audio clips of preachers and politicians and TV judges into their music, turning them into backup singers of a kind. In her report, *The Speech-to-Song Illusion*, Deutsch shares her theory: That our brains suppress musical cues when we listen to people talk so that we don't hear what they're saying as songs, but repetition overrides the suppression, so the music underneath the speech comes through.

The idea puts me to mind of an older, more fanciful theory that I've always sort of loved. During the nineteenth century, philosophers were interested in pinpointing the origins of language. There's one called "the la-la theory" that suggested that human language grew out of its earliest ancestor, music, and that music, in turn, was created spontaneously to satisfy a basic human need to express love and emotion.

The la-la theory, and other ideas like it, have since been brushed off as silly and old-fashioned, but maybe those philosophers were onto something. Maybe music and poetry, language, and love, are all sort of the same thing, all bound up in whatever it is that makes us human. I know I've always liked the idea.

27

How to Become the Media

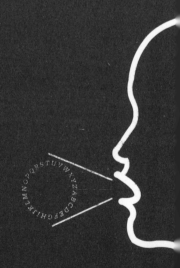

You've never really understood what's up with the anarchist kids—the West Philly squatters and the crust punks who hang out on South Street with their dogs. Then again, when you left for the second annual Underground Publishing Conference (UPC), you didn't know it would be so political.

Jason Kucsma of Become the Media Inc., the group that publishes *Clamor Magazine* and the *Zine Yearbook* and organizes the conference, tells you even he wasn't sure what this year's event would bring. He does say, "The *Yearbook* allows us to see what the underground has printed—and a lot of it is great, and a lot is not so great."

You pack your bags for Bowling Green, Ohio. You'll decide for yourself what's great and what isn't.

The Midwest turns out to be very flat, a parched alien landscape. Bowling Green, described as a college town, is sure enough that and not much else. A friendly girl in a coffee shop (the coffee shop) says the town boasts 18,000 people during the school year, but only half that when the students go home.

Saturday afternoon at the conference is back-to-back sessions. Slither into a crammed classroom during a discussion on the Books Through Bars collective of Philadelphia. A floppy-fauxhawked boy leaps out of his chair so you and your giant backpack have a place to sit. Over the course of the weekend, you'll discover that: a) all the people here are this gentle; b) all the sessions are this packed; and c) Philadelphia keeps coming up.

Moving from session to session, notice how well organized this gathering is. You've seen people behave much worse at professional conferences, the kind sponsored by the corporations that own the White House. The UPC didn't even charge a registration fee.

Watch people mill around outside the classroom. Kids with half an inch of encrusted grime on their bare feet sleep on plastic chairs. A boy with long hair and a t-shirt that reads "Anarchy is our way of life" sits on his feet and reads. Girls with shaved heads and arms full of tattoos greet each other warmly. They haven't seen each other since—oh my God—since Seattle!

Meet a bearded hiker-looking guy with a microphone who runs an anarchist talk show when he's not working on an organic farm. Except for a former Black Panther and a gregarious librarian from the *Utne Reader*, nobody looks older than 25. And even though a zine just informed you that fashion is "fash-ism," you make a mental note that retro green Sauconys look really cute with hot pink socks. You are a consumer pig, caught up in the capitalist machine. Hope no one notices.

Try to keep track of all the projects you learn about. It's not easy. Two librarians from Salt Lake City's main library have started one of the first zine archives in the country. Jim Munroe, whose first novel was published by William Morrow and Co., shares the pleasures of touring with his second, self-published, book on his own shoestring budget. A woman from the Independent Media Center of Chicago insists, "If you've had something political happen to you and you want to talk about it, you're a journalist." Fret a bit about job security.

Three trendy girls from Brown assure everyone that it's easy to produce a radio show as impressive as theirs; decide they're being generous. Julie Herrada, the curator of the Labadie Collection at the University of Michigan, talks about the man behind the largest archive of social protest literature in the world. Plan to go to your own library and learn more about Joseph Labadie, the man they called the gentle anarchist.

Head to the lovely old theater on Main Street that night for two hours of indie films. Scott Beibin of West Philly's Lost Film Collective has brought the Lost Film Festival, and he's clearly delighted. He says "yay!" a lot and wants to know if you're having fun. You are.

He shows a Jerry Springer episode he pranked by pretending to be the guy who slept with the girl whose boyfriend was cheating on her with their roommate. There's a lot of screaming. It's pretty funny. Not everybody appreciates the joke, though. One curmudgeonly punk girl over-enunciates, "WHAT WAS THE POIN-TUH?!"

Laugh anyway.

Fall in love with *The Manipulators*, a two-minute animated film by Andrew Jeffrey Wright and Clare Rojas from Philadelphia's

Space 1026 gallery. In the film, an issue of *Marie Claire* opens to reveal Sharpie drawings that march across ads and fashion spreads. Big snakes appear, eat ladies' handbags, then poop. It seems to encapsulate the weekend's overall sentiment: If you don't like the mainstream, you can reject it. You can make it your own.

Wright tells you, "One of the purposes [of the film] was simply to add imagery and give it a different meaning—to heighten the ridiculousness that is already there." He says he isn't sure what to make of the crustier radical kids either. "No, I'm not an anarchist. I'm an I-don't-knowist."

Wonder how so many interesting people lived in your hometown without you realizing it. Later, ask Scott Beibin, who tells you: "West Philly is like the East Bay of the East Coast. It's a mishmash of anarcho/socialist/green political groups and religious organizations far off the Wonder Bread barometer." He mentions that on his recent U.S. festival tour, people all over the country asked about his neighborhood and used the word McPenntrification. Worry fleetingly about how the rest of the country perceives your town.

But back in Bowling Green, where ATMs are few, you run out of cash by Sunday afternoon. Go from table to table in the vendor room like a beggar and leave with a backpack full of beautiful zines, newspapers, and CDs anyway. Discover that the UPCers' anti-capitalist rhetoric is more than photocopied words on a page. Wonder if these people have looked at a newsstand lately, if they know how precious their ideas are. Feel sad about saying goodbye.

Next to you on the plane home, a skinny woman from West Virginia describes, between sips of beer, the tortures she'd like to inflict on various headline-making criminals. It's her argument against capital punishment, which is "too easy."

Nod and wince and page through your bounty of zines, most of which declare prisons anti-human. Be glad you spent the weekend in Bowling Green. Be glad the gentle anarchists exist. Be glad you have a new word for what you are: An I-don't-knowist. This way, you're always becoming.

Epilogue

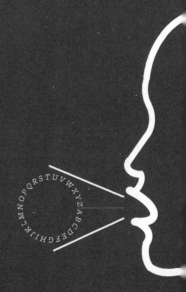

In a few weeks I'll be moving out of the apartment I've lived in for the last nine years. I have a ton of sorting and cleaning to do before I even begin packing because, in the words of a friend who likes stuff as much as I do, "I am not a minimalist."

Yesterday as I was going through things, I pulled six small paintings off the wall and wrapped them carefully in paper; these will definitely make the move to my new place. An old internet friend made them for me; this guy from Ukraine who found me on the lost civilization of Myspace, where I'd made a profile for a zine I used to publish under a ridiculous pseudonym. He did the paintings on the shiny side of shirt cardboards, the ones the dry cleaner puts inside dress shirts to keep them from wrinkling up, and the figures on them look like extinct animals or little monsters of some kind, like the shadow-shapes you saw in your childhood bedroom when you couldn't fall sleep. They're rounded, friendly monsters, not horrible snakey ones, and Yakiv—that was my friend's name—rendered them in dark blue and black with a dab of red or yellow here and there.

Yakiv made a zine too; his was about music. We trades zines through the mail but I couldn't read Russian, the language his were written in, and he grew up in the time before they taught English in school, he said, so even though he'd worked on learning the language he couldn't read the stories I sent him, not really. Over the Myspace email program we tried to talk to each other, maintaining short, broken conversations about the copy shops we used to make our zines, the shitty jobs we both had, and how much we loved our cats who annoyed us by walking on top of us first thing every morning. The stiltedness of our conversation ensured that it was always simple and sweet. And we liked each other, sensed a certain kinship in that mysterious way you can, even though layers of unknowableness—foreign languages and the chill light of computer screens and whole freaking continents—separate you. Eventually I think Yakiv had to admit defeat in the face of this doomed conversation-based friendship: He wanted me to know that he liked me, but he just couldn't talk to me. So he made these dark, witty paintings and sent them to me, and I hung them on my wall.

I was touched that he thought enough of me to make me a gift, but I loved the paintings for other reasons as well. I liked the way they got to the heart of things, that they were there for us when we had no words. I mean, God knows there are plenty of times when language fails us all, and it can lead to all kinds of heartache. Misunderstandings and estrangements, tears of frustration, the secret locked inside your heart that you just can't say. But this time, the inadequacy of language was an occasion for two people, basically strangers, to be much more tender with each other than they might otherwise have been. Yakiv wanted to make friends and he couldn't say so in the way he was used to, so he had to show me. And when I looked at the funny, strange creatures he'd drawn, I understood more about him than he could have told me even if he'd grown up down the street.

I never bothered taking down that Myspace profile, but for the life of me I can't remember what old email address I might have used to log into it. It looks like Yakiv hasn't used his in years anyway, and Google searches for his name and his zine don't bring up anything anymore. Even in our small, modern, digital world, my old friend seems too far away to reach.

Maybe it doesn't matter now anyway. The paintings on my wall still have volumes to say, every time I look at them, and I think that's probably enough. I mean I guess it would be neat to write to him now and tell him how much I've treasured his gift, but what would I say? That I think his drawings are cute? That I've never forgotten our brief, long-distance friendship, and in fact have thought of it often? Everything I can think to tell him is either too much, or not enough.

SUBSCRIBE TO EVERYTHING WE PUBLISH!

Do you love what Microcosm publishes?

Do you want us to publish more great stuff?

Would you like to receive each new title as it's published?

Subscribe as a BFF to our new titles and we'll mail them all to you as they are released!

$10-30/mo, pay what you can afford. Include your t-shirt size and month/date of birthday for a possible surprise! Subscription begins the month after it is purchased.

microcosmpublishing.com/bff

...AND HELP US GROW YOUR SMALL WORLD!